# WOMEN SILVERSMITHS
## 1685-1845

# WOMEN SILVERSMITHS
## 1685-1845

*Works from the Collection of*
*The National Museum of Women in the Arts*

PHILIPPA GLANVILLE

JENNIFER FAULDS GOLDSBOROUGH

THE NATIONAL MUSEUM OF WOMEN IN THE ARTS

Washington, D. C.

in association with

THAMES AND HUDSON

1990

To Lorraine and Oliver R. Grace,
whose generosity made this catalogue possible

Editor: Brett Topping

Silver Photography: Arthur Vitols, Helga Photo Studio, New York City

Copublished by Thames and Hudson and The National Museum of
Women in the Arts, Washington, D.C.

© 1990 The National Museum of Women in the Arts

Library of Congress Catalog Card Number 89–51744

Printed and bound in Japan

Front cover: *Portrait of Louisa Courtauld* by Johann Zoffany (1733–1810).
(Courtesy of Sir Julien Courtauld)
Back cover: One of a pair of George III tea caddies by Louisa Courtauld
and Samuel Courtauld I, 1766.

# Contents

# Acknowledgements

This book represents the culmination of many months of commitment and effort on the part of numerous individuals. On behalf of the Board of Directors and staff, we wish to thank first Lorraine and Oliver R. Grace, whose generosity made this catalogue possible. We are extremely grateful to the members of the Grace family and their friends, who joined together to donate the remarkable collection of works by women silversmiths to The National Museum of Women in the Arts (NMWA) in honor of Lorraine Grace: Mr. Gerald I. White, Mrs. Anne G. Kelly, Mrs. Lori Grace, Mrs. Wendy Grace, Mrs. Ruth Jervis, Mr. and Mrs. Joseph Claps, Mr. Steven Kull, Mr. David Grace Charry, and Mr. Oliver R. Grace. Later Mrs. Colin Brown, Faith Corcoran, and Carol and Denis Kelleher very kindly contributed additional pieces. We also thank Nancy Valentine, who had the foresight, knowledge, and determination to assemble the collection.

The essayists for the catalogue, Philippa Glanville and Jennifer Faulds Goldsborough, along with the scholars who compiled the extensive appendix, Biographical List of British and Irish Women Silversmiths, deserve high praise. We thank Barbara Ward for her time spent in discussing possible essayists. We are also grateful to Timothy Kent for his generosity in sharing his research on women silversmiths from the former county of Wessex in England.

Brett Topping, who edited the catalogue with great care and devotion, has done an outstanding job. We thank our excellent Communications Department intern Jennifer More for her many contributions to this book. We are also grateful to Jane Walsh and Mary Kay Davies from the Smithsonian Institution for their assistance, as well as staff members Torrance York, Susan Sterling, Elea Kemler, and Nancy Lutz.

We also wish to thank those who assisted in making this catalogue what it is. Arthur Vitols spent many hours photographing the silver to produce such splendid images. George T. (Ted) Dalziel from the National Gallery of Art Library helped greatly in locating comparative illustrations. Elaine R. S. Hodges, a scientific illustrator with the Smithsonian Institution, drew the wonderful hallmark reconstructions included in the Collection Checklist. Finally, we are grateful to all of the institutions and private collectors that allowed us to reproduce their art.

Rebecca Phillips Abbott
Deputy Director

# Introduction

## NANCY VALENTINE

This catalogue was developed thanks to the generosity and enthusiasm of Lorraine and Oliver R. Grace. It documents the silver marked by women in the collection of The National Museum of Women in the Arts and is the first book to focus on the subject of women silversmiths, bringing to light their important and long participation in the silver trade in Britain and Ireland.

Most people are surprised to learn that women worked as silversmiths, marking everything from spoons to massive ceremonial pieces. Because of the practice of registering a maker's marks at the local assay office of the goldsmiths' guild and the careful records kept at the Goldsmiths' Hall in London, however, it is easy to establish that women worked as silversmiths and also to learn their names.

The biographical appendix to this book lists well over three hundred women who registered their own mark or became apprentices to silversmiths between the late 17th and mid-19th centuries. Researched and compiled by Catherine Drillis, Philippa Glanville, and myself, this extensive list demonstrates women's largely unrecognized participation in the silver trade. We hope it will serve as a valuable resource for future scholarship on the subject.

The title of the catalogue—*Women Silversmiths, 1685–1845*—is consciously similar to that of one of the great resource books on the subject of English silver, Arthur Grimwade's *London Goldsmiths, 1697–1837: Their Marks and Lives*. This catalogue, however, concentrates on women from all of the United Kingdom and covers a slightly broader period, determined by the earliest and latest years that women represented in the museum's collection registered their marks—Elizabeth Haselwood most probably registered her mark in 1685 and Elizabeth Eaton entered hers in 1845.

I often am asked how I began the collection of objects by British and Irish women silversmiths which has been given to The National Museum of Women in the Arts by Lorraine Grace, her family, and friends. My story is similar in some ways to that of Wilhelmina Holladay, who established the museum itself. Independently and in our different fields we found beautiful objects made by women artists and artisans. We become curious, looked for more information, and started to collect. In only five years' time I was able to assemble over one hundred silver pieces made between 1695 and 1852 and hallmarked by thirty-five different women. I achieved this through a single-minded purpose and by attending almost every major silver auction in New York. My great interest in developing the collection was to find pieces attributed to as many different women makers as possible to demonstrate how many women worked in the field. I also wanted to collect a wide variety of objects and styles to show the types of pieces that were in popular use and the designs that were stylish in the 18th and 19th centuries. This made my project an exciting treasure hunt.

My interest in silver dates back to my teenage years, when I bought a Mexican tray for my mother. At the same time I made frequent visits to the Marshall Fields store in Chicago to admire their antique Irish silver with my knowledgeable friend Adelaide Read Hunker. My desire to collect lay dormant for twenty years, however, as I was working with and writing about plastics as an art form. Later, watching a friend in Bermuda put together, piece by piece, a wonderful tea caddy spoon collection, I learned a great deal about 18th-century English silver. At this point my husband, Richard Valentine, suggested that I, too, invest in some antique silver.

Financed by my husband, and my friends Bill Agnew, Faith Corcoran, Lorraine Grace, Louise Healey, Denis Kelleher, Bill Panke, Bernard Selz, Fred Stein, and Jeff Tarr, I began buying Georgian silver. I happily realized that buying antiques at auction was an interesting way to study history, do detective work, and enjoy the excitement of a "game of chance." Because I now lived within walking distance of the top auction houses in New York, I was able to spend hours studying each piece at the auction previews. Christopher Hartop, Jane deLisser, and Anthony Phillips at Christie's became trusted friends, advisers, and allies over the years.

As I started purchasing pieces of silver I began to come across names like Dinah Gamon and Elizabeth Jones. I realized that pieces by women were rather undervalued at auction sales. Soon I was concentrating on buying Georgian silver made by women.

Consulting various sources in the field, I found the names of 141 women whose marks were registered from 1370 to 1850.[1] Over one hundred of these women were working in London. Others were registered in Barnstaple, Birmingham, Bristol, Chester, Exeter, Hull, Newcastle, Norwich, Sheffield, Dublin, and Cork. Many were widows whose initials were often enclosed in the traditional diamond-shaped mark, following the heraldic practice of enclosing a widow's coat of arms in a diamond-shaped shield. Immediately, however, I discovered exceptions to this rule, such as Hester Bateman. She marked her silver with a feminine *HB* in script.

In addition to the 141 women silversmiths, I learned of women apprentices from two articles by E. J. G. Smith published in the *Antique Dealer and Collectors' Guide* in 1969. This source mentions 142 young women who were apprentices, listing by name 19 who completed their apprenticeship and were given their "freedom," meaning they were fully qualified silversmiths. Unfortunately, they did not register their marks, so there is no way of identifying their work. They may have been employed as journeymen, or may have married and changed their name, being known to us now by their married name.

One of my most exciting acquisitions was a tobacco box made by Elizabeth Haselwood of Norwich *ca.* 1695. The box, one of forty-four surviving pieces of silver made by Haselwood, was formerly on exhibition at the Norwich Castle Museum. Norwich also honored Elizabeth Haselwood by presenting Queen Elizabeth II with a piece of her silver.

Having the decorative arts libraries of the Metropolitan Museum of Art and the Smithsonian's Cooper-Hewitt Museum nearby was a great help. I soon learned that silversmiths were not merely artisans. Silversmithing was one of the few socially acceptable trades in which a gentleman could engage. In some cases trustworthy silversmiths acted similarly to bankers, assisting in cash transactions or serving as safe depositories. Often, too, patrons would bring unfashionable or broken pieces of silver to be melted down and recrafted, sometimes leaving them to accumulate for future use.[2]

At the libraries one of the first books I found was David Shure's *Hester Bateman, Queen of English Silversmiths*. This history chronicles Bateman's rise to prominence as a highly successful woman silversmith of the 18th century. Born in poverty, she not only continued the family business after the death of her husband but expanded it and became quite wealthy. She was active for many years, working into her eighties. Under the supervision of Hester and several family members who were also silversmiths, the Bateman workshop produced a great quantity of attractive, practical, and moderately priced silver objects.

Other books were equally helpful. Arthur Grimwade's scholarly study of records at Goldsmiths' Hall, mentioned previously, contained drawings of marks and biographies of over one hundred women silversmiths who lived and worked in London from 1697 to 1837. It was also interesting to find women's trade cards pictured in Ambrose Heal's *The London Goldsmiths, 1200–1800*. Looking carefully at Elizabeth Godfrey's cards, I was thrilled to realize that I had purchased two Godfrey sauce boats very similar in design to a sauce boat depicted on one of her trade cards.

As the collection took shape I had the desire to share it with others. I viewed it not as a lavish display of individual objects but as an expression of how women lived and worked in the 17th, 18th, and 19th centuries. I loaned several pieces to the Bayly Art Museum of the University of Virginia in Charlottesville and continued to collect more pieces, which I loaned for a while to the President's House at Mount Holyoke College. I also wrote the article "Women Silversmiths of the 18th and 19th Centuries, Part I and Part II" for *Silver* magazine (November–December 1984; January–February 1985).

It was at this time that Wilhelmina Holladay and I met and discussed the possibility of housing the entire collection at the soon-to-be-inaugurated National Museum of Women in the Arts. My dear friend Lorraine Grace, who showed confidence in me from the beginning, contributed funds to the museum to buy the collection and display it properly. Without her generosity and that of her family and friends, none of this would have been possible. We are also indebted to Faith Corcoran, Carol and Denis Kelleher, and Mrs. Colin Brown for adding to the collection.

The rewards of collecting with a focus are many. Not only does it make a collection stronger, it also helps develop a network of knowledgeable and interesting acquaintances. The process of assembling a collection of silver objects marked by women gave me great pleasure, but it has proven equally rewarding to see these lovely works displayed at The National Museum of Women in the Arts and included in this important museum catalogue.

*Notes*

1.   Generally, the silver made in England has four marks: the sterling content, the maker, the year in which it was made, and the city in which it was assayed. The mark verifying the sterling content of the silver was touched by the assay office of the Goldsmiths' Company, as required by the law regulating the making of silver objects.

2.   It is reasonable to assume that silver shops were family operations and that masters would have their wives and children helping. Many silversmiths had their homes and workshops under one roof or next door to one another.

# Women and Goldsmithing

## PHILIPPA GLANVILLE

She seeketh wool, and flax, and worketh willingly with her hands. . . .
She perceiveth that her merchandise *is* good; her candle goeth not out by night. . . .
She maketh fine linen, and selleth *it*; and delivereth girdles unto the merchant. . . .
Let her own works praise her in the gates.

Proverbs 31

Businesswomen are not 20th-century phenomena. Women of competence, determination, and appropriate business skills have been essential to economic life as far back as the first written records. The prototype for Chaucer's Wife of Bath—a woman of property, widowed more than once, who managed her finances skillfully enough to be independent—was a common figure in medieval English society. For centuries in the City of London, as elsewhere, women administered their property and ran businesses during widowhood. It was often after the death of her husband that a woman came into her own and assumed a new identity.

Many women were active business partners with their husbands, however. One example of a woman who contributed greatly to the family trade was the enterprising Mrs. Bland, a naval provisions merchant much admired by Samuel Pepys. "Above all things pleased to hear Mrs. Bland talk like a merchant in her husband's business very well, and it seems she do understand it and perform a great deal," wrote Pepys on December 31, 1662. Nearly two years later, on September 8, 1664, he noted, "Fain to admire the knowledge and experience of Mrs. Bland, who I think as good a merchant as her husband."

Despite the mocking reference to the presumed frailty of women made by playwright Mary Manley a generation later in her prologue to *The Lost Lover* (1696)—"To Fringe and Tea they should confine their sense"—women did play a crucial role in the economy of London. Peter Earle's recent study of the middle class in late Stuart and early Georgian London, *The Making of the English Middle Class, 1660–1730*, shows that about one third of all women of property ran a business. London's unmarried women lived by their own work and made up more than ten percent of the women taking out insurance policies on business premises. Many of the women engaged in business in the 17th, 18th, and 19th centuries were involved in the silver trade.

Descriptions of women goldsmiths have often taken one of two extreme positions. The first is that a few outstanding women were uniquely gifted as artisans, suddenly emerging in widowhood with previously untried skills. Hester Bateman is the most exaggerated example of this misconception, thanks to a thoroughly misleading biography. The second, equally

Opposite: (*Fig. 1*) A charming custom relating to silver that continued into the 19th century was for milkmaids to dress in their best clothes on May Day and dance for their customers. They carried a headdress adorned with silver tankards, plates, and other silver objects to add to their allure. The engraving *The Merry Milk Maid* (ca. 1688) is from a design by Marcellus Laroon the Elder (1653–1702) and was included in the series *The Cryes of the City of London*. (Courtesy of the Museum of London)

untenable, position is that the mark of a woman meant nothing more than the most nominal connection with her late husband's business. The true picture, as always, is more complicated.

By the 17th century, if not long before, the goldsmiths' trade had become very diversified. To think of either women or men as goldsmiths without knowing the context in which they worked, therefore, is unhelpful. What is or was a goldsmith? The convenient portmanteau term originated with the craft title to which a citizen free of (i.e. admitted to full membership of) the Goldsmiths' Company could lay claim. This was the title he or she used for personal identification in documents of all kinds, even wills. This apparently straightforward term concealed an enormous range of activities related to the precious metals, however, from banking to refining, from casting to retailing. These distinct enterprises had their own names. Other more specific and descriptive terms, such as plateworker, goldworker, largeworker, or smallworker, were employed for artisans within the craft in the 18th century. The term *goldsmith* also encompassed the work of a silversmith. By the mid-18th century in London, *goldsmith* implied a retailer as well as a member of the Goldsmiths' Company, while *silversmith* referred to a manufacturer or artisan.

Certain activities by their nature identify the main creator responsible. The names of female artists, such as the popular Stuart portraitist Mary Beale (*ca.* 1632–99), the Swiss painter Angelica Kauffmann (1741–1807), who had a successful career in London in the 1760s and 1770s, or the rococo silk designer Anna Maria Garthwaite, are remembered not merely because of the quality of their work, but because they signed pieces which have been preserved. They also corresponded with fellow artists and patrons and functioned in a cultural group which took pleasure in its literacy, creating paper records of activities and expenditures. Contemporary comments by diarists, references to commissions in account books, even membership in the Royal Academy of Arts, all document their lives and work.

Many engravers are also known by name, since they normally signed or initialed their pieces. This craft was closely linked to the goldsmiths' shops because engravers often worked to order in silver. A few names of women engravers are recorded in English sources. For instance, we can identify Magdalene Van de Passe, a member of a distinguished family of engravers originally from Utrecht. She and her brothers worked in London. Her brother Crispin Van de Passe is known to have produced signed portraits on silver of English nobility and of the families of James I and Charles I.

Once we enter the world of the goldsmith, however, very few pieces can be attributed to women or men. In England, as in France, goldsmiths' work was virtually never signed. The only exception to this general rule occurs in Holland in the early 17th century, when members of the Van Vianen family sometimes signed their work, thereby claiming parity with sculptors. The only identifying mark on silver is the maker's, or more properly the sponsor's, which has its own restrictions and difficulties and whose purpose frequently has been misunderstood.

In the past the initials or devices marked on English silver were assumed to identify the maker. Now, as craft and business records are analyzed, it is becoming clear that the people who designed, raised, or chased a piece—in effect, its creators—often had no direct responsibility for the object and, indeed, no direct connection with the person affixing the mark. In fact, the mark well might be that of a retailer, who bought finished silver objects from a whole series of subcontractors.

Fortunately, thanks to the survival of records for one large, fashionable Georgian business, that of John Parker and Edward Wakelin (1759–77), the retailing of silver can be examined in detail. Two series of records from their business have survived—the Gentlemen's Ledgers, showing what their clients ordered, and the Workmen's Ledgers, naming all their subcontractors, who were well-known specialists in one or another aspect of manufacturing silverware. When the clients' orders are checked, it becomes clear that virtually every item sold to a client came from subcontractors or suppliers, although many of them are struck with the marks of Parker & Wakelin. The enterprise of Parker & Wakelin had a mark, therefore, but no workshop. Thus the term "maker's mark" ceases to be accurate and merely confuses any discussion about who actually made a silver object.

The retailers' practice of buying from specialist suppliers was undoubtedly in full swing earlier in the 18th century. Often the retailer overstruck the supplier's mark. A candlestick in the Victoria and Albert Museum, for example, has Elizabeth Godfrey's mark overstriking that of her supplier, whose own mark is unreadable. This practice was carried on outside London, as is revealed by the 1802 tea caddy by Newcastle upon Tyne goldsmith Ann Robertson in the collection of The National Museum of Women in the Arts. Robertson's mark also overstrikes that of an indecipherable supplier (see Collection Checklist). The practice of overstriking explains the existence of identical pieces with different marks—a single workshop probably was supplying various retailers. When the owner of a retail business also ran the workshop, the fact was sometimes stressed on trade cards, with phrases like "working goldsmith" or "made in workshop," implying direct responsibility for the objects produced.

Occasionally, on late 18th- and 19th-century flatware, a tiny extra mark appears, identifying the outworker responsible for the particular batch, but these marks are normally quite anonymous. The responsibility for the finished piece of silver was widely diffused and many individuals could claim a part in its creation: from the hammerman (always male) through the raiser, chaser, or engraver (usually male) to the burnisher (often female). All had a hand in the final appearance of an object, but only the master, who probably had less physical contact with the silver than any of them, can usually be named.

By the late 18th century the division between manufacturing silversmiths, often employing outworkers, and retailers was clearly established. Some retail businesses, such as that of Parker & Wakelin or Thomas Heming (active 1745–post-1773), stand out for their size. They used their own marks, thus concealing their suppliers' identities. The largest Regency business, Rundell, Bridge & Rundell (1805–39), had a fashionable shop in Ludgate Hill and owned two workshops managed by Benjamin Smith and Paul Storr in other parts of London.

This distinction between manufacturer and retailer was emphasized on important orders when retailers engraved their name and address prominently on the object, overshadowing the initials of the manufacturer. An elaborate vase with candelabrum branches at the Los Angeles County Museum of Art, made in 1824 by Rebecca Emes and Edward Barnard, the partnership running the largest manufacturing business of the early 19th century, is engraved prominently around the base with the retailer's name: FISHER BRAITHWAITE & JONES FCT (FCT comes from the Latin *fecit*, meaning "made it"). This vase (figs. 2, 3, and 4), like much of Emes's and Barnard's presentation silver, is modeled on a design by Piranesi after an antique marble vase. The cost of this enormous piece (it weighs over 1,200 ounces) was £895 17s. 2d., and the ledger entry shows that the makers charged the high rate of 14s. an ounce for it.

The responsibility of both Rebecca Emes and Edward Barnard in their enterprise was: to employ good draftsmen, chasers, modelers, and engravers; to negotiate with the retailers who

Above: (*Figs. 2 and 3*) Two details of modeled frieze in high relief on the main body of the SILVER VASE WITH CANDELABRUM BRANCHES by Rebecca Emes and Edward Barnard.

Above right: (*Fig. 4*) SILVER VASE WITH CANDELABRUM BRANCHES (*ca.* 1824) by Rebecca Emes and Edward Barnard. (Courtesy of Los Angeles County Museum of Art—The Arthur and Rosalinde Gilbert Silver Collection)

were their clients; and to maintain their extensive provincial and overseas network. Their ledgers show that they shipped goods up to York, where they were overstruck with the mark of a local York retailer, to Exeter, to Ireland, and to India, for sale in Calcutta. The world of Rebecca Emes or of Louisa Courtauld was that of the leading business owners in England, who dealt personally with retailers, as well as with their royal and noble clients.

Courtauld was a prominent member of one of the most famous families of English goldsmiths. As Ambrose Heal records in *The London Goldsmiths, 1200–1800*, when her associate of many years, George Cowles, printed his own trade card he referred to himself as "late partner with Mrs. Courtauld." Louisa Courtauld's portrait was painted by Johann Zoffany (fig. 5) who also painted members of the Royal Family. Judging from her dress and demeanor in this lovely picture, the compass of her daily activities was far removed from the workshops upon which her prosperous way of life ultimately was based.

At another economic level entirely were the women who lived by the labor of their hands, often as finishers or burnishers. They were paid weekly wages or by piecework. Another low-grade and low-paid task, often carried out by women, was the making of silver and gold buttons. "A pretty ingenious business, it requires no great strength . . . [women] . . . work for a mere trifle and hawk their work about the trade at an under price," notes R. Campbell in *The London Tradesman*. The earnings of women in the precious metal trades were lower than those of men in the same occupations. In 1770, however, Arthur Young noted that, in the relatively new trade of silverplating in Sheffield, women and girls earned "very good wages, much more than by spinning wool," from 4s. 6d. to as much as 9s. a week. On his visit to Birmingham twenty years later, he found the women's wages "higher than in any place in Europe," 4s. to 20s. per week. The rates paid to women recorded in Matthew Boulton's papers are at the lower end of this range. For instance, Elizabeth Allen's agreement to work "at burnishing and

(*Fig. 6*) *Burnishing*. Reproduced from *British Manufacturers: Metals* by George Dodd (1845).

polishing" (fig. 6) for Boulton and Fothergill for two years in 1769 quoted a rate of 4s. a week. Seven-year-old girls were employed in the Birmingham toy trade in 1759, but they were earning as little as 1s. a week.

Apprenticeship was not customary in the new industrial towns of the Midlands, and girls as young as ten or twelve were found working in shops a century later, in 1862, by the Parliamentary Commissioners investigating the conditions of the children employed in silversmithing and silverplating in Birmingham. The evidence quoted by John Culme in his study of 19th-century silver gives fascinating details of working conditions. The hours worked by girls of seventeen or eighteen were normally 8:00 am to 7:00 pm. At William Hutton's shop in Sheffield, girls were earning between 3s. and 14s. per week. They had set times for their meals and somewhere to wash and change, "no men being allowed in their rooms." The activities of these young women—plating, buffing, and coloring plate with a mop and rouge—were unskilled and far removed from the traditional picture of the goldsmith as artist/craftsperson. Figures from the 1841 census for occupations, which covered England, Wales, the Channel Islands, the Isle of Man, and vessels in the Royal Navy, indicate that there were substantial numbers of women employed in the precious metals. The total number was over 360. Of all of the women working in silver, one-sixth were under twenty.

Fire insurance policies taken out by women who described themselves as goldsmiths demonstrate a great diversity in the type and size of their business, with extremes of wealth and poverty. At the top end were the "toywomen" like Mary Deards, who supplied fancy goods and novelties made of gold and silver to a fashionable clientele. Another example is Catherine Riccard, whose premises and stock in Leicester Fields were insured for £3,000 in 1787. At the other extreme was Mary Wynn, who struggled to continue as a goldsmith and pewterer at the rather dismal address of Execution Dock, Wapping. Her entire stock and goods were insured for a mere £200 in 1781.

By ancient custom of the City of London, a person who was apprenticed and became free of one of the livery companies could practice any other craft within the city and its environs, run a workshop, or open a retail shop and take apprentices. In the 17th century, if not long before, *goldsmith* simply designated a member of the Goldsmiths' Company, who might have absolutely no working trade connection with gold and silver at all. Conversely, a working goldsmith might be free of another company or guild. Paul Storr, for instance, is now known to have been apprenticed through the Vintners' Company, presumably because his father was a vintner, and Thomas Jenkins, a prominent retailer of goldsmiths' wares in the time of the later Stuarts, described himself as "Free Butcher."

Women followed the same pattern. Dor Scrivener was a free cutler who probably registered a mark as a smallworker in 1697. There are, as Arthur Grimwade has noted, at least forty-four other London livery companies of which practicing goldsmiths were members. Because of this practice, and for other reasons considered later, the Registers of Largeworkers and Smallworkers at the Goldsmiths' Company cannot give a completely accurate or comprehensive census of the craft, nor even its active members. Only those masters who had occasion to register a mark at the Assay Office are named. Even the list of these marks published by Arthur Grimwade is incomplete, since the Registers used do not commence until 1697 and two are missing from the 18th-century series. The Smallworkers' Register for the period from 1739 to 1758 is missing, as is the Largeworkers' Register covering 1758 to 1773. There is an earlier copperplate struck with marks from about 1675, but the parchment

18

strips signed with the markers' names disappeared long ago. Informed speculation by Gerald Taylor and Timothy Kent, as well as references from other sources have enabled a few of the missing pre-1697 names to be identified. Some names have been associated with previously unattributed or misascribed London marks in Arthur Grimwade's *London Goldsmiths, 1697–1837: Their Marks and Lives* (3rd edition in preparation). Even for London, however, there will always remain some unidentified or merely attributed marks, and the provincial goldsmiths offer similar, if not more complex, problems. The new edition of Charles Jackson's fine reference book, *Silver & Gold Marks of England, Scotland & Ireland* (1989), reproduces many more marks which are found on silver but are not yet identified.

In the major provincial towns the picture is more patchy than in London. In 1423 seven towns (Bristol, Coventry, Lincoln, Newcastle upon Tyne, Norwich, Salisbury, and York) were appointed as assay towns, each with a town mark. Documents pertaining to their silver industry before the late 16th century are rare, as are examples of silver objects produced in these towns. A century before the Britannia Standard Act of 1697, other towns, such as Exeter and Chester, had come to the fore. Their goldsmiths, many of whom went to London as apprentices, set up organizations parallel to that of the London goldsmiths and began using a town mark, date letter, assay mark, and maker's mark. Little correlation can be made between the names of these goldsmiths and their marks, since the copperplates struck with marks survive only rarely. There are sufficient documentary references, nonetheless, to enable a reasonably complete census of goldsmiths in Chester, Exeter, Newcastle, Norwich, and York. Elsewhere in England and Ireland goldsmiths were active in virtually every town, and distinctive marks can sometimes be associated with goldsmiths known to have worked in the region. In Wessex Timothy Kent has identified many marks, as have Mrs. G. E. P. How in Bristol, Brand Inglis in King's Lynn, and Geoffrey Barratt in Norwich.

After the Britannia Standard Act of 1697, new arrangements for hallmarking became necessary and the Wardens of the Goldsmiths' Company rode out from London to enforce the new regulations in the provinces. With the passing of the Provincial Assay Office Act of 1701, the provincial goldsmiths found it advantageous, if not essential, to sell wares struck with the full marks, either those of London or of the nearest regional assay office. Few provincial pieces of the 18th century have makers' marks only, whereas before the Britannia Standard Act it had been common practice to strike the maker's mark repeatedly and no other mark, as on the spoon made by Mary Sweet of Crewkerne (fig. 7).

In 1773 the shift of manufacturing away from London to new commercial centers in the Midlands and the northern provinces, coupled with skillful lobbying by Matthew Boulton, led to the extension of the assay to Birmingham and Sheffield. The official Registers of marks are virtually complete from that time and recent studies of the London, Birmingham, Exeter, and York goldsmiths have exploited these sources and shown how diverse the occupations of the women in the trade could be. In Birmingham, for instance, in the first thirty years of the 19th century, women were running businesses as silvercasters (Ann and Elizabeth French with William Jones), bucklemakers (Mary Platt) and spurmakers (Jane Timmins). In London Mary Godley, widow of Benjamin, continued their business of silver flatting (producing sheet silver from ingots). She insured her goods and the valuable flatting mill in Bagnio Court off Aldersgate Street for £1,000 in the 1770s.

Women were normally in a position to register a mark only on the death of a husband already active in the craft. The essential ingredients of a successful silver business were a team of

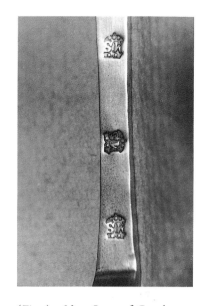

(*Fig. 7*) Mary Sweet of Crewkerne stamped her initials several times on this spoon, using no other marks. Prior to the introduction of the Britannia standard, this was a common practice among provincial silversmiths. The spoon has a pricked date of 1697.

skilled craftsmen, a stock of dies, patterns, and molds, a good foreman and shop manager, strong credit, and satisfied customers. None of these were attributes which necessarily vanished on the death of the master goldsmith, assuming that there was a successor with energy, determination, and business acumen.

The marks of widows were often set within a lozenge, the traditional heraldic device for a widow, as were Sarah Holaday's marks of 1719 and 1725. Elizabeth Buteux, whose three-lobed mark entered in 1731 incorporated her husband's peacock device, later remarried and registered as Elizabeth Godfrey in 1741, with her second mark in a widow's lozenge. If a woman remarried, she vanished again behind the identity and mark of her new husband, often the manager or senior journeyman in the workshop. Dorothy Mills, widow of Hugh, was in partnership with Thomas Sarbitt in Saffron Hill, London, from 1746 to 1749. The collection of The National Museum of Women in the Arts has a sauce boat from 1748 jointly marked by Mills and Sarbitt and at Williamsburg, Virginia, there is a pair of salvers from 1752 with their joint mark, although she registered a separate mark as a largeworker that same year. By December of 1753 she had married Thomas, however, and thereafter marked her works Dorothy Sarbitt.

The usually brief period of independent identity during widowhood before remarriage should not be interpreted as the total sum of the woman's commercial and craft activity, which probably started in a minor way in her late teens in her father's workshop and continued until marriage. Her separate identity was then lost during a tacit partnership with her husband, only to re-emerge on his death. Widows who did not remarry registered marks that show they often carried on in business for as long as twenty or thirty years. Hannah Coley was the daughter of a bucklemaker. She married Thomas Northcote and registered a mark on his death ten years later, in 1798. She remained active in the craft almost until her death in 1831. Rebecca Emes, widow of John, was a partner first with her husband's executor, William Emes, in June 1808, perhaps as a legal convenience in sorting out her husband's estate. In October of that year she entered a mark with Edward Barnard. She registered her fifth mark with Barnard in October 1825.

Where partnership was succeeded by marriage, it may be that the male partner had been the workshop manager. Mary Ann Hyde registered a smallworker's mark as a partner of John Reily in November 1799. Later she married him, and he entered marks alone from 1801 to 1826. She re-emerged as Mary Reily in partnership with Charles, presumably her son, on John's death in 1826. Hyde had taken out an insurance policy in her own right on premises in Carey Lane after her first husband's death. Anne Smith's partnership with Nathaniel Appleton as smallworkers in 1771 did not mean that she lost her independent existence. She also took out an insurance policy on her premises and stock as a silversmith.

Elizabeth Pantin, daughter of the distinguished Huguenot silversmith Simon Pantin, married twice, both times to active goldsmiths. Her first husband, Abraham Buteux, was from the French immigrant community. Her second husband was Benjamin Godfrey. The business dealings of her father and successive husbands indicate that they were supplying the nobility with high-quality silverware, often with a strong French flavor. She had two periods of independent activity in widowhood, the second when the rococo style was sweeping through the decorative arts of England and forcing artisans to adopt new styles. The clientele of the business she ran remained loyal, providing evidence of her ability to manage a business and respond to the prevailing fashions in silver. That Elizabeth Godfrey's clients included a royal

duke, earls, minor nobility, and others of discrimination and wealth is suggested by the heraldic images incorporated in one of her trade cards (fig. 8). She undoubtedly takes the crown as the outstanding woman goldsmith of the 18th century.

Dual-career families often occurred in the silver trade. When the husband was a silversmith, perhaps a smallworker, the wife might well have her own occupation in a related specialty. Margaret Binley, for example, appears in the Workmen's Ledger of Parker & Wakelin as a supplier of pearl buttons and silver buckles, products typical of the small-scale luxuries for which women workers were often responsible. It was only after her husband's death that she registered her mark in 1764 to continue running their workshop which produced wine labels.

The women who registered marks were a minority of those engaged in the craft, as the biographical list demonstrates. Names of women were only recorded in the Minute Books and Apprenticeship Registers of the Goldsmiths' Company (and to a lesser extent in those of other livery companies) if they were apprenticed and subsequently made free, or, later in life, if they registered a new mark or took an apprentice. The other occasions for women to be brought to the attention of the Court of Wardens arose if they were found committing a craft offense or if they needed a pension in widowhood. Further documentary sources are sketchy and the discovery of women goldsmiths is a matter almost of happy chance rather than systematic search. The names of women goldsmiths who ran their own businesses appear as holders of insurance policies in London and the provinces. As Ambrose Heal demonstrated many years ago, trade cards and advertisements are a good source of information on goldsmiths, both women and men. The bills, account books, and correspondence of other goldsmiths and of their clients also provide insights. For instance, the order books of the Newcastle firm of Beilby & Bewick have survived. These ledgers record the transactions with Mary (Mercy) Ashworth of Durham, active between 1785 and 1803, who sent work to be engraved by them.

It is easier to discover details about all of these women who were active in their own right than about the hundreds of women who were employees or outworkers. The names of the latter can be retrieved only if the wage books of a business survive. Very few do, since these have been considered merely as ephemera until very recently. A printed billhead for Louisa Courtauld was used for invoicing four second-hand dessert spoons in the 1760s. The shop assistant who signed the receipt on behalf of Courtauld and her company was a woman—Judith Touzeau—a fellow Huguenot and fellow parishioner of her mistress. The letter book of the goldsmith and jeweler George Coyte at the Victoria and Albert Museum, which contains his business correspondence, indicates that he dealt with female suppliers in the 1770s.

A century earlier, in the 1660s, an anonymous goldsmith entered payments to women in his Day Book virtually every week. These anonymous smallworkers were employed at piece rates for chasing and other tasks, such as thimble making. Like so many of their fellow silversmiths, their work was not marked and they may well have served no formal apprenticeship, merely learning their skill in their father's workshop and carrying it on into their married lives. The unnamed goldsmith's records were seized by the Court of Chancery and are now in the Public Record Office, London.

Frequent references are made to women who took an active part in their husbands' business in the records of the Goldsmiths' Company until the mid-18th century, when the company gradually began to relinquish its close control over the craft. An early regulation of 1399 referring to women arose from the need to protect the secrets of the craft; it required that no member of the company should give any goldsmiths' work to a woman who was married to a member of another trade. If such a transaction took place, a fine of 6s. 8d. was payable and the informer was to be rewarded with 20d. Not only were wives of other tradesmen considered unreliable, but often the goldsmiths' wives themselves acted as convenient scapegoats for an offense committed against the sterling standard. Such was the case of John Gislingham in 1653. An ingot of silver which had been sent from his shop to be made into wire at the "Wyer Office" in Great St. Helens was found to be below standard. His wife was blamed because she had "caused some silver to be cast into an ingot during my absence." His wife's partnership was clearly an active one. When his silverwares were found wanting, his wife paid the fine (5s.) and collected the offending articles, which were, as she pointed out, made by someone else altogether, who should take the blame.

Women who registered their own mark were treated like male goldsmiths in every respect, including being taken to task in their own right by the Court of Wardens for any deficiencies in their work. Such actions were, in fact, an indication of the normality of women's participation in the silver trade. The Minute Books of the Exeter Goldsmiths' Company, for instance, contain letters exposing the maneuverings of Mrs. Elvie, a silversmith of Dartmouth. In 1708 she sold some substandard spoons to the Exeter Assay Master, who was making an inspection of goldsmiths' shops in the region. She did not deliver them to him, however, realizing that the poor quality of her work would bring her into disrepute. This was not a new experience for her, since nine years before, in 1699, she had been caught by the Wardens of the London Goldsmiths' Company selling substandard plate. Her letters of 1708 in reply to the Exeter Wardens' complaint were clearly equivocal, and she substituted better spoons. The company wrote back, "not withstanding yu pretend to womanly weakness, we find you have tricked us men a second time, for these are not ye spoons which were bought of yu." She was threatened with prosecution at the next Sessions, but history does not relate whether the company pressed the charge or whether she was treated leniently.

Women goldsmiths were active in every county of Britain and Ireland, though they were concentrated in London. Local sources do not produce comprehensive lists of all those gainfully employed in the goldsmiths' trade, however, and women were not always given due recognition, whatever their contribution to the business. Sometimes women do not appear in the records kept by the assay offices in the area but are included in the Minute Books of the London Goldsmiths' Company, which have similar entries regarding male goldsmiths from the provinces.

Susan Light, wife of the Bristol goldsmith John Light, traveled to London in 1683 to represent her husband before the London Wardens on a charge of selling substandard plate. She was clearly successful in her appeal, since she managed to have the £4 fine reduced to 20s., on account of the alleged poverty she and her husband endured and the traveling expenses she had incurred.

A wife who was an active manager might be an inconvenience, however, as William Lyle of Southampton discovered. When the London Wardens visited the town in 1631 they were obstructed from entering his shop. As a result, they decided to impose a fine which was eventually reduced when they were satisfied that the delay "proceeded more by the obstinacy of his wife than of himself."

A good deal is known about the enterprising wife of Thomas Dare the Younger of Taunton. Thomas Dare, the son of a leading Taunton goldsmith, also Thomas, was born in 1644. He married Ellen Knight in the late 1660s, and his two younger sons both subsequently followed their father and grandfather into the goldsmiths' trade in Taunton. Thomas Dare himself was unwise enough to become embroiled in the tempestuous politics of the 1670s, however, when Charles II was resisting petitions from all over the country calling for Parliament to sit. Convicted of speaking seditious words, Dare was fined £500 and imprisoned until he paid. Subsequently, in March 1680, he escaped to Holland, where he became closely associated with and paymaster to James Scott, Duke of Monmouth. After the death of Charles II in February 1685, he returned to England as part of Monmouth's invasion. Meanwhile, his wife had been running the business in Taunton. Dare had taken the precaution of transferring his property to trustees in Taunton and making a will with specific provisions for the continuity of his goldsmithing business. His trustees were to ensure that Ellen should have the use of certain sums of money without having to pay interest while she ran their business as a widow. A steady flow of cash was, of course, essential for any goldsmith, particularly one located in a provincial town without a community of neighboring goldsmiths to call upon for resources.

Ellen Dare continued to run the business in Taunton, presumably with the help of her two younger sons, John and James. In June 1699 she had to travel to London to appear before the Wardens at Goldsmiths' Hall for selling substandard goods. She was charged 10s. 7d. (the value of the goods) and fined 8s. 5d. Her business thrived. She used Thomas Dare's mark, even before his death in 1685, and, subsequently, a cinquefoil mark. Her firm also apparently employed subcontractors among Taunton's working goldsmiths, such as Samuel Dell and Richard Hamlin. The objects themselves attest to the subcontracting process. A number of laceback trefid spoons of the 1690s have been found, all with designs struck from the same die but each bearing the mark of Dare, Dell, or Hamlin. Such dies were costly and may have been the property of Ellen Dare, who had the largest business of the three. She lived until February 1739 without remarrying, surviving her husband by more than half a century.

A long and active widowhood may have been more common among the women goldsmiths outside London, where there were fewer goldsmiths from whom they could choose a second husband to create a stronger trade partnership. Esther Forbes, widow of the Dublin silversmith Robert Forbes, registered three marks between his death in 1718 and her retirement in 1729. Elizabeth Hayward of Salisbury continued her husband Thomas's business after his death in 1677 and was still active twenty-two years later, when she was fined by the London Goldsmiths' Company for trade offenses. Mary Roberts of Bristol and Mary Ashe of Launceston had even longer records. Roberts was active from approximately 1679 to 1715. Ashe was the widow of Richard Ashe, who died in 1689. She carried on their business until her death in 1722. Her mark is recorded in the Minute Books of the Exeter Goldsmiths' Company in November 1703, but another mark which may be hers—an *A* over a star—has been found on Launceston spoons from a decade earlier.

Thanks to Margaret Gill's careful study of local newspaper advertisements, the careers of Newcastle goldsmiths are well documented. Dorothy Langlands continued her husband John's large business from 1804 until she retired in 1814. It comprised two quite distinct sections—the retailing side and the manufacturing side. For the shop and counting house she advertised for "a person accustomed to the silver and jewellery business," with impeccable references. For the manufacturing aspect she required skilled journeymen and apprentices. The two areas of her business used different skills, although both were classed as goldsmithing.

In 1726 Daniel Defoe wrote *The Complete English Tradesman*, a description of the occupations of London, with advice to parents about the suitability of different professions for their children. In chapter 23 he describes the goldsmiths' trade, like that of linen drapers, mercers, and "dealers by commission," as "not proper for the women to meddle in." He adds that as a result of long-standing custom and women's opinion of these businesses, "we never or rarely see any women in such shops or warehouses." His recollection is inaccurate and misleading, however, for at the time he was writing—that is, within the first thirty years after the commencement of the new Register of marks at Goldsmiths' Hall in 1697—about forty women goldsmiths were active in London. These women had taken on their deceased husbands' businesses and registered marks. They were women as prominent as Alice Sheene, who supplied a handsome matching coffee and chocolate pot to the Ironmongers' Company in 1706. The women recorded at Goldsmiths' Hall were, as mentioned previously, only a small percentage of the women actually engaged in the craft, just as masters were always a small proportion of the working male goldsmiths. Many other women's names could be added, such as Ann Jaquin who was made an apprentice in 1723 and never married. Working as an

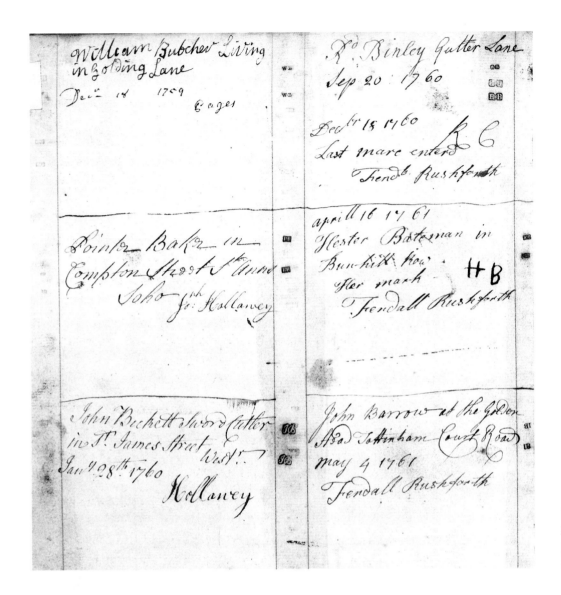

(*Fig. 9*)   First register entry for
Hester Bateman on April 16, 1761.
(Courtesy of the Worshipful
Company of Goldsmiths)

employee, she became free of the Goldsmiths' Company many years later. She took her
freedom in 1746, many years after entering the craft, presumably because the workshop
manager had died or moved on, and she needed the right to take apprentices. She took on a
female apprentice, Elizabeth Bence, within a year whose actual occupation, however, may not
have been concerned with silver.

Ann Jaquin probably belonged to a lower social class than the better-known women who
were the daughters of goldsmiths and later registered marks themselves. Anne Tanqueray, the
first child of David Willaume, was born in 1691. She did not marry David Tanqueray until
she was twenty-six, after at least a decade of close collaboration with her future husband who
was completing his apprenticeship to her father. Her own workshop was later located near the
main family establishment in St. James's, and she cooperated with her brother on large orders,
such as the massive rococo centerpiece recently acquired by Temple Newsam House, Leeds.

The education and training given to the daughters of London merchants and tradesmen is
harder to describe than that of the daughters of gentlefolk and the nobility due to the lack of
adequate documentation. Some had the opportunity of attending boarding schools in the
suburbs of the city, a custom which went back to the Middle Ages. In 1673 the prospectus and

curriculum of Basua Makin's school at Tottenham High Cross consisted partly of languages and partly of dancing, singing and music, writing and keeping accounts. She was attempting to reform the normal curriculum for girls, which laid much greater emphasis on skill with the needle than proficiency in languages. Hannah Woolley, as well as many writers on women's education and employment in the 17th and 18th centuries, was deeply concerned with the limited opportunities offered to girls, and deplored the new aspiration to gentility shown by the daughters of tradesmen. Defoe later made the same observation. He noted that a wife not versed in her husband's business might find, upon her husband's death, that she had to cope with an unscrupulous shop manager or other unpleasant matters. "This I mention for the caution of those ladies who stoop to marry men of business, and yet despise the business they are maintained by; that marry the tradesman but scorn the trade."

The Goldsmiths' Company differed from other guilds in requiring that masters teach their apprentices to read and write, a valuable addition to the normal craft skills. A few daughters of goldsmiths were apprenticed through the Goldsmiths' Company. Records indicate that 19 young women completed their apprenticeships between 1614 and 1845, but an additional 142 girls were apprenticed.

Sadly there is no way of determining which practical aspects of the business were undertaken by these young women. Presumably well spoken, presentable, and literate, they were capable of serving customers in the shop. The often-quoted inability of Hester Bateman to sign her name next to her mark in the Goldsmiths' Register (fig. 9) is extremely unusual, and only a handful of women registering marks at Goldsmiths' Hall had to use a device rather than their signed names. The daughters of Huguenot households certainly, and other women probably, could speak and write in French. Paul Crespin and David Willaume both habitually used French in corresponding with their clients and in annotating their accounts, although the shop manager drew up the original bills in English. An account presented to Lord Monson by Paul Crespin is annotated with a receipt signed by the goldsmith's wife, Mary Crespin. Trade cards were normally printed in French and English, among the fashionable retailers at least. For instance, Ambrose Heal reproduces the card of William & Mary Deards/Guillaume et Marie Deards. French silver was greatly admired and ideas for new designs often were inspired by French engravings. It was a distinct advantage for a goldsmith to be bilingual.

Campbell's *The London Tradesman*, published in 1747, offered similar advice as that given by Defoe to the parents of daughters, stressing the advantages for women of the specialized dress-accessory trades, such as the manufacture of gold and silver buttons or lace. For the father, the cost of a daughter's apprenticeship was considerable, particularly to the goldsmiths' craft, which was far costlier than any other apprenticeship, as Campbell notes. In the mid-18th century the fees ranged between £30 and £60, but John Collyer in his *Parents and Guardians Directory* of 1761 quoted as much as 200 or 300 guineas as a premium payable for entry to a fashionable, successful business. These were sums which a father would hardly be inclined to pay for a daughter's education, if she could acquire good training at home without formal apprenticeship. Such apprenticeships, however, gave access to a wider range of opportunities, including marriage and investment. Apprenticeship of women died out by the early 19th century, a casualty of the general decline in the traditional craft structure of London.

By the ancient custom of the City of London, young men were not permitted to become free, to marry, or to own property until the age of twenty-one at the earliest. The period before coming of age allowed time to complete an apprenticeship, which started at any age between twelve and sixteen and normally ran for seven years. It also offered the chance to acquire experience by working as a journeyman. In addition, the postponement of marriage increased the possibility of accumulating some capital and gaining the trust and confidence of a master. Women also tended to defer marriage to their mid-twenties. Hester Bateman married at twenty-four, an age which enabled her to acquire sufficient experience and business knowledge for her future work. Daughters of goldsmiths, presumably unmarried but independent, very occasionally appear in the Minute Books of the Goldsmiths' Company, such as "Mr. Presson's daughter" of Wood Street. She was caught in 1653 selling silver seals, "Coarseales," which were not up to the sterling standard.

Given their undoubted energy and commitment to the family business, as revealed by their continuing engagement in the craft during widowhood in many cases, women members were given remarkably little formal recognition by the Goldsmiths' Company. Occasional entertainment was provided for these women, particularly for those married to the members of the Court of Wardens and Court of Assistants. For example, a coach was hired for the Wardens' wives attending Mrs. Sherriff at a Guildhall Feast on New Year's Day in 1661. In 1765 the Court of Wardens provided a river trip, a dinner, and a day out for the gentlemen of the Court of Assistants and their wives. They also gave a ball (but not supper) in November or December of 1765 for the same group. This custom was dropped in 1781 because of a hurricane in the West Indies, "thereby preventing an improper appearance of festivity."

Widows whose husbands had been members of the Court of Wardens or Court of Assistants were accorded a degree of honor in the Goldsmiths' Company Minutes, but women had no access to the offices of the company nor could they belong to the Court of Wardens, until the 20th century. They worked, in effect, without a vote and without a voice in the policy-making activities of the Goldsmiths' Company, despite the fact that those policies affected their interests.

In a short study such as this, one can hope to do little more than clear away some misconceptions about the role played by women in the craft of goldsmithing and draw attention to interesting areas for future investigation. Many questions remain to be answered: the nature of the training women received; whether Huguenot women had advantages over native Londoners; whether women were admitted to the Society of Working Goldsmiths (a trade club active in the 18th century); whether at any period men and women were equally rewarded for their work; and whether the advent of industrialization, particularly the increase of large-scale production, benefited or disadvantaged women. Claims have been made on both sides, often based on a simplistic, even sentimental, view of what women themselves wanted from life.

What can be stated definitively, however, is that women played a pervasive role in the goldsmiths' trade from its inception. As the records of the industry and other documentary sources attest, women participated at nearly every level of the business, from retailer to rouger, shop manager to apprentice. Indeed, they undoubtedly contributed greatly to many of the other guilds, such as the weavers', silkmakers', and provisioners'. By uncovering the details of women's work in the goldsmiths' trade, therefore, we gain greater appreciation of the vital role they have played through the centuries in the economic history of Great Britain and Ireland, and, by extension, that of many other countries.

*Sources*

The library at Goldsmiths' Hall in the City of London is the starting point for any study of British goldsmiths. Here the company's archives are preserved, including the Minute Books of the Court of Wardens and Court of Assistants, the Apprenticeship Books and the Registers of Largeworkers and Smallworkers. Printed sources for the history of the Goldsmiths' Company include Walter Sherburne Prideaux's *Memorials of The Goldsmiths' Company* (2 vols., 1896–97) and Thomas Fiddian Reddaway's and Lorna E. M. Walker's *Early History of The Goldsmiths' Company, 1327–1509* (1975). A history of the company during the 16th and 17th centuries is in preparation.

The history of hallmarking is fully and clearly described in Susan Hare's *Touching Gold & Silver: 500 Years of Hallmarks*, a catalogue of an exhibition held at Goldsmiths' Hall in 1978. Marks of London goldsmiths and short biographies are published in Arthur Grimwade's *London Goldsmiths, 1697–1837* (1976), and John Culme's *The Directory of Gold and Silversmiths, Jewellers and Allied Traders, 1838–1914* (1987). In 1935 Ambrose Heal published shop signs and trade cards in *The London Goldsmiths, 1200–1800*. Arthur Young's four-volume work *A Six Months' Tour through the North of England* (1770) provides valuable insights into conditions outside London.

Since Alice Clark's *Working Life of Women in the Seventeenth Century* (1919) and Ivy Pinchbeck's *Women Workers and the Industrial Revolution, 1750–1850* (1930), pioneering studies of English women at work, the attention given to women goldsmiths has been patchy and has inevitably focused on their marked products. Fifty years ago Joan Evans discussed women goldsmiths briefly in "Huguenot Goldsmiths of London," *Proceedings of the Huguenot Society* (1936). In 1946 the indefatigable Edward Wenham published "Women Recorded as Silversmiths," *The Antique Collector*, vol. 17 (March/April 1946), and more recently Eric J. G. Smith wrote two articles—"Women Silversmiths—Part I" and "Women Silver-smiths—Part II: Hester Bateman"—adding further names. They appeared in *The Antique Dealer and Collectors' Guide*, vol. 23 (May 1969) and vol. 23 (September 1969).

The policy registers of the Sun Fire Insurance Company, deposited at the Guildhall Library, are a rich source of information about both London and provincial policyholders. Nominal indices for the precious-metal trades are kept at Goldsmiths' Hall and in the Department of Metalwork, Victoria and Albert Museum. In addition, I am grateful to Timothy A. Kent for access to his partly unpublished research on Wessex goldsmiths. For other counties, see the Select Bibliography.

Peter Earle's *The Making of the English Middle Class, 1660–1730* brings to light many interesting facts about women's ownership of property in the 17th and 18th centuries.

An essay drawing on Helen Clifford's study of Parker & Wakelin appears in the *Handbook to the International Silver and Jewellery Fair, London* (1990).

A recent general book on silver by the author, which concentrates on the social and economic history of craft organization, is entitled *Silver in England* (1987).

# Silver by British and Irish
# Women Silversmiths
# in the Collection of
# The National Museum of Women in the Arts

## JENNIFER FAULDS GOLDSBOROUGH

*The history of silver*

Silver has been valued highly since the dawn of metallurgy for its natural properties. Its basic atomic and molecular structure make it especially malleable and ductile. It does not oxidize or combine readily with other materials to cause unpleasant or poisonous substances. Exceptionally sanitary, it is easily maintained, durable, and adjusts to changes in temperature more quickly than any other metal. Its gleaming, reflective surface provides visual and tactile pleasure. The value and usefulness of silver have led silversmiths* to enhance the metal's natural luster with their own carefully crafted shapes and decorations.

The natural properties of silver make it ideally suited for serving food and beverages. In the centuries before the introduction of porcelain and high-grade ceramics, plastics, stainless steel, and other miracles of modern technology, silver played an essential role at the dining table. It was a luxury item because of the rarity and expense of the raw ore. Its position as a status symbol derived from its serviceability, however, as much as from its aesthetic appeal.

Silver is the archetypal reusable material, and much of the metal available to 18th- and early 19th-century silversmiths in Europe, Great Britain, and Ireland was also used by the ancient Greeks and Romans. The metal had been melted down and recycled repeatedly. The store of silver in Europe was significantly increased after the early 16th century by ore shipments from Spanish America, however, prompting major changes in the silver trade.

The British silver industry expanded dramatically during the second half of the 17th century. Changes in land usage and foreign trade, particularly with the Far East and America, greatly increased the availability of money. Silver was imported from Spanish America literally by the ton, meaning that its price fell while personal income was rising. By the 18th century the great quantity of the metal on the market and its gradual reduction in cost in real terms made silver utensils accessible to a much larger population. Objects started to appear in a wider range of styles and in varying quality throughout the 18th century. The introduction of Sheffield plate in the 1750s made silver objects even more affordable. By the mid-19th century, with the invention of the inexpensive electroplating process and the tremendous influx of raw silver from

---

* In this essay *silversmith* is interchangeable with *goldsmith*.

mines in the western United States, the purchase of solid or silver-plated objects became a possibility for many British and Irish families.

In its pure state silver, like gold, is too soft to endure much use. However, the addition of small amounts of other metals, such as copper, enormously enhances its strength and versatility. What we call solid silver is actually an alloy. There are dozens, if not hundreds, of silver-alloy formulas. For centuries the alloy most widely used in England has been called sterling—92.5 percent pure silver combined with 7.5 percent copper mixed with trace metals.

Silver has been made into coins from early times because it is valuable even in small quantities and can easily be cast or struck into standard units. Since coins can be melted down and made into objects, and silver objects, in turn, can readily be fashioned into coins, many governments have regulated the quality of the alloy used by silversmiths, to protect the value of their currency. In Great Britain this regulatory power has been invested in the goldsmiths' guilds. In England the Guild of London Goldsmiths was incorporated in 1327. The Worshipful Company of Goldsmiths in London, an expanded corporation with perpetual succession, was chartered in 1462.

The regulatory marking of silver in England began prior to the incorporation of the London guild, however. The leopard's head mark, which guaranteed the purity of the alloy, was introduced in 1300. By 1363 makers were required to have a personal mark which they stamped on their work. Since then additional marks have been added to indicate the year in which a piece was tested for purity and to designate the recognized assay office at which the test took place. Between 1784 and 1890, when special taxes were levied on silver products, a fifth mark was used to certify that the duty had been paid. The strict compliance with these regulations makes it possible for collectors and scholars to determine with ease where, when, and under whose auspices a piece of English silver was made. For centuries these early laws protecting the consumer have assured that the clients of English silversmiths have received work of a high standard.

Silver was so rare throughout Europe after the fall of Rome that it was reserved for the use of God through the established Church and, by extension, for royalty through the divine right of kings. Church silver had to be awe-inspiring, exquisitely crafted, and imbued with conventional symbolism. Silver for the Crown had to be pompous and gorgeous. It also had to attest to the power, wealth, erudition, and sophistication of the ruler. To meet the exacting demands of silver clients during the Middle Ages and the Renaissance, silversmithing became the élite preserve of a few extraordinarily gifted and highly educated men. Conversant with the latest silver-crafting techniques and the most original forms of reinterpreting classical styles, these silversmiths were also highly familiar with the accepted iconography and visual symbolism of Christianity. The rare works of art they produced were used by relatively few people and had little impact on styles of domestic silverware.

As a result of the expansion of the British silver industry in the late 17th and early 18th centuries, the middle class could afford useful household objects of silver for the first time. The silver market, formerly governed by the needs and taste of the aristocracy and the Crown, now started to respond to the preferences of a wider clientele. The demand for simple spoons, cups, and dishes was met by increasing numbers of competent artisans. It was no longer necessary for all silversmiths to be capable of producing impressive ecclesiastical or royal presentation wares.

Many shops began to specialize in one or two types of silver. To meet the ever-growing market, wives and other female relatives of a master silversmith were pressed into service—

frequently into the more routine jobs, such as engraving and polishing. Widows of silversmiths with such experience found that they were able to continue running shops with the help of journeymen or partners. A few women were even accepted as apprentices, artisans, and entrepreneurs in their own right. While most women continued to enter the craft in association with fathers, husbands, brothers, or sons, it became unnecessary to indicate such affiliation by the shape of their mark.

To compete in the silver trade successfully, women silversmiths had to maintain the same high standards of craft and awareness of fashion as their male peers. A few shops continued to accept royal and sacred commissions for exceptional silver, demanding the highest degree of artistic achievement. Most silversmiths, however, including a number of talented women, joined the ranks of those producing the quantities of attractive, stylish, functional silverware that has delighted households, collectors, and curators for the past two centuries.

A piece of silver can reveal much about the background and standing of its maker and the way of life, status, and tastes of its original owner. It can also suggest characteristics of the larger society of which it forms a part. Taken as a whole, this collection amply demonstrates that the women who marked the objects were aware of the latest styles and were highly quality conscious. There is nothing to suggest that these pieces were the work of women, either individually or collectively. Indeed, they are more indicative of the tastes and social standing of the clientele than of the owners of the silver shops that produced them. On the whole, the silver is distinctive for its conservatism, simplicity, and middle-class appeal rather than for its sophistication. Stylistically, it tends to be typical of its period and form. The artistry embodied in these pieces leads to the conclusion that women silversmiths probably found it expedient to pay careful attention to the quality of their product. Whether working as business managers or taking a more active role in the craft itself, women silversmiths undoubtedly were assured of greater success by producing styles of proven popularity than by attempting to experiment with new ideas.

It is perhaps worth noting that much of the work in this collection looks very familiar to American eyes because it is exactly the sort of silver which was within the financial reach of the provincial American consumer. Similar objects were sent to America in some quantity, serving as inspiration and models for local silversmiths.

## The objects in the collection

### 1. Drinking vessels

The earliest and most ubiquitous silver objects are beverage servers. Silver drinking vessels, derived from the form of cupped hands or other such natural containers as cows' horns, have changed very little in shape over thousands of years. Silver cups—with or without feet, handles, or covers—meet a universal and timeless need.

The earliest drinking vessel in this collection is also one of the most complex in form. It is a large tankard marked in 1706 in London by Alice Sheene (pl. 1). Tankards —large cylindrical drinking vessels with hinged covers, hollow scroll handles and capacities ranging from a pint to a quart—were one of the most common forms made in silver throughout most of the 18th century. The tankard was a communal drinking vessel in domestic use for serving the everyday household beverages of ale, beer, and cider. Unlike 19th- and 20-century ceramic beer

steins, which resemble tankards but which have become associated with men, tankards were frequently gifts to women upon marriage or following childbirth. This latter custom is touchingly depicted in a German drawing from the mid-17th century by Jonas Arnold the Younger (fig. 10).

The rather square proportions of this tankard are consistent with its relatively early date. Mid-bands and shallow, domed lids were popular on straight-sided English tankards between about 1710 and 1730. This form provided the model for slightly later, American-made silver tankards from the Philadelphia area, whose 18th-century silver closely resembled English prototypes. The presence of the sponsor's mark on the handle (appropriate for tankards made before the reign of George I) indicates that the hinge, despite being slightly too large for the handle, is an original feature. The cover, which also looks as though it could be a later addition, is marked as well. The finely engraved coat of arms in the baroque style is original, too.

So much currency was melted down to be used by goldsmiths for plate during the Restoration years (1660–88) that the required standard for wrought silver was raised by a parliamentary act of 1696–97 from the traditional sterling alloy to a new standard of 95 percent purity to prevent the easy transformation of coins to objects. The new alloy prevailed until 1720, when its use became optional. Called the Britannia standard, it could be recognized by a mark representing the female allegorical figure of Britannia. Silver made of the Britannia standard, of which the Sheene tankard is an example, was more valuable than sterling because of the higher silver content. It was also softer and, therefore, subject to greater wear and damage. Consequently, few pieces of Britannia standard silver have survived.

Another interesting drinking vessel in the collection is the 1719 two-handled cup which carries the mark of Sarah Holaday (pl. 2). It, too, is made of rare Britannia standard alloy, the softness of which is demonstrated by the small crack in the rim and the reinforcing disks at the lower handle joints. The applied wire mid-band and rim, as well as the particularly graceful, broken-S-scroll handles, enhance the simple, inverted-bell shape which was common from approximately 1700 to 1765. The two-handled cup was useful for holding any beverage but was particularly popular for hot caudle and posset—drinks similar to eggnog. Larger versions of this form were made with deeply domed covers. Such cups, which made impressive presentation gifts, were the forerunners of 19th-century loving cups and modern trophies. During the 17th and 18th centuries it was customary to display the more elaborate examples of two-handled cups on tiered sideboards or cupboards to demonstrate wealth and patronage.

(Pl. 1)  QUEEN ANNE TANKARD
WITH COVER, Alice Sheene,
London, 1706. This tankard is the
second Britannia standard piece in
the collection. Its handle terminates in
a heart engraved with a coat of arms.
Sheene is one of the earliest London
silversmiths whose work survives
today. She marked this tankard with
the first two letters of her surname in
a widow's lozenge and also a tiny
heart. (Height: 7¼ in.)

(Pl. 2)  GEORGE I TWO-HANDLED
CUP, Sarah Holaday, London, 1719.
This cup is made in the simple,
inverted-bell form out of the soft,
Britannia standard alloy used between
1697 and 1720. It has a particularly
nice patina and shimmery, planished
surface. Cups such as these, which
often had covers, were used for
communal drinking and pledging
"healths." (Height: 5¾ in.)

(*Pl. 3*)  GEORGE III GOBLET, Ann Bateman and Peter Bateman, London, 1797. The graceful, attenuated lines and mirror-like surface of this piece are typical of neoclassical silver. (Height: 6 in.)

Opposite: (*Pl. 4*)  Drinking punch was a favorite male pastime during the 18th century. The GEORGE III DOUBLE BEAKER (1790) on the right by Hester Bateman could be used as a traveling cup or for drinking parties away from home. Elizabeth Cooke's GEORGE III SALVER (1767) was used to serve wine glasses such as the GEORGE III GOBLET (1797) by Ann and Peter Bateman. The GEORGE III TODDY LADLE (1802) by Elizabeth Morley has a twisted bone handle which floats, making retrieval easy should it slip into the punch. The GEORGE III SNUFF BOX (1802) is by Alice and George Burrows.

The maker's mark on both the Holaday cup and Sheene tankard is indicated by the first two initials of the surname, according to the requirements of the Britannia standard, which were in force from 1697 to 1720. The practice continued on Britannia standard silver until 1739.

Goblets are simply drinking cups raised on a stemmed foot. Western cultures seem to associate height with elegance and importance, so the addition of a tall stem is an easy way to enhance what might otherwise be an undistinguished vessel. The West has considered wine to be the most refined beverage since Greek times and earlier. The goblet, therefore, which is the most elegant of all silver drinking vessels, has always been associated with the service of wine. When used in an ecclesiastical setting for Communion, the goblet is called a chalice. Very large, ornate, silver and silver-gilt goblets were fashionable during the 16th and 17th centuries, but were replaced by glass (for wine) or silver tankards and two-handled cups (for less notable beverages) during most of the 18th century.

Silver goblets enjoyed something of a revival between about 1780 and 1825, and this collection includes two excellent examples from the early and late phases of that period. Like much Bateman silver, the 1797 goblet marked by Ann and Peter (pl. 3) has a timeless simplicity. The somewhat attenuated oval bowl on a plain, funnel-shaped foot is typical of neoclassical silver at its most severe, and closely resembles the Scandinavian style of the 1950s and 1960s. This cup is made of a very thin gauge of silver, with all extraneous ornamentation and detail omitted.

34

Historically, fashion follows a repetitive cycle of taste ranging from classic, graceful
simplicity to baroque, sculptural, massive ornamentation. Although still inspired by antique
forms—the Roman *campana*, or inverted bell shape, to be precise—the 1812 goblet marked
by Rebecca Emes and Edward Barnard is representative of the early 19th-century revolt against
neoclassicism (pl. 5). The shorter stem and deeper body with its protruding lobes, as well as the
sharply everted rim, give the Emes goblet a more horizontal look than the Bateman example,
though it is, in fact, only slightly smaller. The baroque play of light and dark in the lobing of the
Emes goblet is echoed in the Greek palmette border on the foot. Comparing the weight of these

two pieces, the lower, sturdier-looking Emes goblet indeed weighs almost half as much again as the Bateman piece. This more substantial quality was both a feature of the new style and a requirement for attracting a more affluent clientele.

Rebecca Emes and Edward Barnard incorporated two bands of milled or stamped grapevines in their handsome mug to achieve a stylishly ornamental, massive look (pl. 6). The small, decorated-script initials engraved on this mug are characteristic of works produced around 1814, when the piece was hallmarked. Many mugs of this period were christening gifts. The usual inexpensive ornamentation for such pieces consisted of two bands of horizontal reeding or grooving resembling barrel hoops. The matted panels on the handle of the Emes example and the fine parcel gilding place it in the category of exceptional, high-style craftsmanship.

Emes and Barnard also produced a more unusual cup carrying the date letter for 1825 (pl. 7). This coconut-shell cup with silver mounts was probably intended for decorative or commemorative purposes rather than actual use as a drinking vessel. Such exotic objects as coconuts, seashells, and antique carved bowls have been mounted in silver as cups since medieval times. Although the popularity of these curiosities diminished during the 18th century, this cup demonstrates Emes's and Barnard's awareness of this long-standing tradition.

The double beaker in the form of a barrel, which was marked by Hester Bateman in 1790, is a particularly charming and inventive drinking vessel (pl. 10). Although rare, this style also was made by other silversmiths toward the end of the 18th century and was a reinterpretation of 16th-century vessels. This object was intended to be used while traveling. When the cups were joined together (fig. 11), the interior could be filled with other dining paraphernalia, such as a folding knife, fork, and spoon. Gentlemen, whether traveling, hunting with neighboring squires, or serving as officers on the field of battle, were expected to provide their own dining and drinking equipment. The rather small capacities of these two cups made them suitable for wine or spirits. Objects such as these also accompanied men on their grand European tours, as demonstrated by Thomas Patch's lively caricature painting of 1760 depicting Lord Grey and his friends in the midst of a drinking party at a Florentine inn (pls. 8 and 9).

2. Drinking accessories

Punch was the lubricant for the wheels of 18th-century social life. A strong drink of inordinate popularity, it was consumed at all times of the day and night by large groups and solitary individuals. The name itself provides a clue to the standard recipe, since the word *punch* is derived from an Indian word for five. Each gentleman took pride in concocting his own secret recipe, but all punch was based on a mixture of rum, sugar, lemons, water, and an aromatic spirit, such as arrack, for flavoring. The preparation and consumption of punch required specialized equipment. Silver, which is relatively unaffected by alcohol or citric acid, was an ideal metal for strainers like the one marked by Sarah Buttall in 1771 (pl. 11), or the toddy ladle marked by Elizabeth Morley in 1802 (pl. 12).

Strainers which could be clipped onto silver or porcelain punch bowls were popular on both sides of the Atlantic. Sometimes the delicately feathered scroll handle was elongated and duplicated on the opposite side of the strainer so that it could be suspended across the punch bowl. Lemon juice, refined sugar, and spices were filtered through the symmetrical and decorative holes.

A potent drink similar to modern whiskey sours, daiquiris, or old fashioneds, punch was served in small quantities. When a few drinkers were to be served, the bowl itself was simply handed around as a communal vessel. To serve large numbers, the liquid was ladled into cups or stemmed wine glasses. Wine glasses of the 18th century were small, holding no more than four fluid ounces. Punch ladles also were small. Their bowls often were hammered out of a single coin, with a socket attached to hold the handle. The shafts of the handles were cleverly made of turned wood or, in the case of the Morley ladle, twisted whalebone, which floated to the surface of the punch. Silver-handled ladles with large, deep, hemispherical bowls, such as the 1796 example marked by Ann and Peter Bateman (pl. 14), were intended for serving soup.

Opposite: (*Pl.* 7) GEORGE IV SILVER-MOUNTED, TWO-HANDLED COCONUT CUP, Rebecca Emes and Edward Barnard, London, 1825. A curious throwback to the silver-mounted cups crafted from exotic materials which were characteristic of the Middle Ages and the Renaissance, this piece combines "antique" and fashionable stylistic features. In all probability, this cup primarily had a decorative or ceremonial function. (Height: 4⅜ in.)

Above left: (*Pl. 8*) and detail left (*Pl. 9*) *A Punch Party: A Caricature Group with Lord Grey* (1760) by Thomas Patch (*ca.* 1720–82). The painting records a gentlemen's drinking party which took place at a Florentine inn during Lord Grey's tour of Italy. In it we see silver traveling cups, a punch bowl with a silver ladle, and other drinking accessories. (Courtesy of The National Trust, Dunham Massey— Stamford Collection; Photo Angelo Hornak)

Above: (*Pl. 10*)  GEORGE III DOUBLE BEAKER, Hester Bateman, London, 1790. These traveling cups join together, forming a barrel shape. The lathe-turned interiors may have been fitted with folding cutlery. Gentlemen of the day were expected to provide their own dining and drinking equipment when traveling or visiting. (Height joined together: 6 in.)

Left: (*Fig. 11*)  GEORGE III DOUBLE BEAKER by Hester Bateman. Cups joined together.

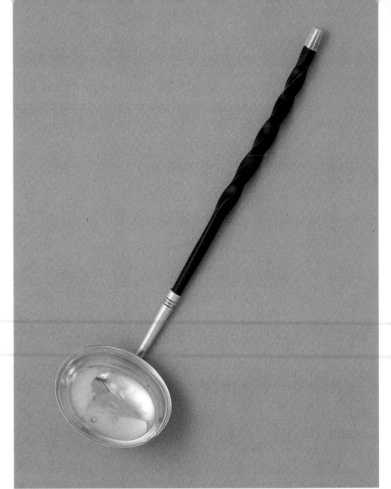

Both the Buttall strainer and the Morley punch ladle are standard, useful objects whose relatively low cost made them available to anyone affluent enough to serve punch. Pieces similar to these might have been sold in any silver shop in the English-speaking world.

Other works in this collection related to sociable drinking customs include a selection of late 18th-century wine labels, also called bottle tickets, marked by Susanna Barker and Margaret Binley, who specialized in making such items. These identification tags were hung around the necks of the heavy wine bottles of the period, which were made of dark-green glass. Wine was not set out on the table during dinner but was served by the glass from a sideboard until the meal was over and the ladies withdrew. At that time men began their serious drinking, and an astonishing number of wine bottles passed repeatedly up and down the table. In numerous 18th- and early 19th-century depictions of men at the dinner table following a meal, there are more bottles than diners! To prevent the rough pontil marks on the bottles from scratching the polished table top and to expedite the passage of the spirits, the bottles were set into coasters with felt bottoms, such as the pair from 1823 marked by Rebecca Emes and Edward Barnard. The grooved wooden interiors of the coasters could withstand damage from the bottles and did not cling to their damp surfaces. Japanned tin or silver rims added an attractive flourish. Coasters often were made in large sets, or at least in pairs, and were usually set at the corners of the table when they were not in use. Pairs of coasters were occasionally made into miniature silver wagons or boats on hidden castors to enable the wine bottles to be passed from one end of the table to the other more easily. As it became customary in the 19th century to transfer wine to decorative crystal decanters, the rims of coasters became more flared and heavily ornamented to show off the sparkling glass. Like much of the silver in this collection, these bottle tickets (pl. 15) and coasters (pl. 16) are typical of their period.

Opposite:
Above left: (*Pl. 11*)  GEORGE III LEMON STRAINER, Sarah Buttall, London, 1771. A small clip near the handle allowed this strainer to be attached to the side of a punch bowl and used when mixing citrus juices, sugar, and spices into the concoction. (Diameter: $4\frac{1}{8}$ in.)

Above right: (*Pl. 12*)  GEORGE III TODDY LADLE, Elizabeth Morley, London, 1802. The light, twisted whalebone handle floats, making the ladle easy to retrieve from the punch. (Length: 7 in.)

Below: (*Pl. 13*)  *The Brothers Clarke with Other Gentlemen Taking Wine* (ca. 1730–35) by Gawen Hamilton (ca. 1697–1737). A servant carries wine glasses on a silver salver to the resplendently attired Clarke brothers and their friends gathered together to drink wine. (Courtesy of the Yale Center for British Art—Paul Mellon Collection)

(*Pl. 15*)  GEORGE III WINE LABEL (left), Margaret Binley, London, *ca.* 1775. Pierced for "Hermitage," a red wine. Silver wine labels or bottle tickets were more elegant than the later paper labels. (Height: 1⅜ in. with a 3-in. chain) GEORGE III WINE LABELS (first three from right), Susanna Barker, London, 1792. Pierced for "Madeira," "Port," and "W. Wine." Madeira and port were particular favorites of the English. (Height: ⅞ in. with 5-in. chain)

(*Pl. 16*)  PAIR OF GEORGE IV WINE COASTERS, Rebecca Emes and Edward Barnard, London, 1823. Coasters such as these protected a table from scratches and drips, and also eased the movement of bottles from one end of the table to the other, a particularly vital consideration for gentlemen's drinking parties. The grooved wooden interiors kept the coasters from clinging to damp bottles and the central silver disk provided a space for armorials or initials. (Diameter of each: 6 in.)

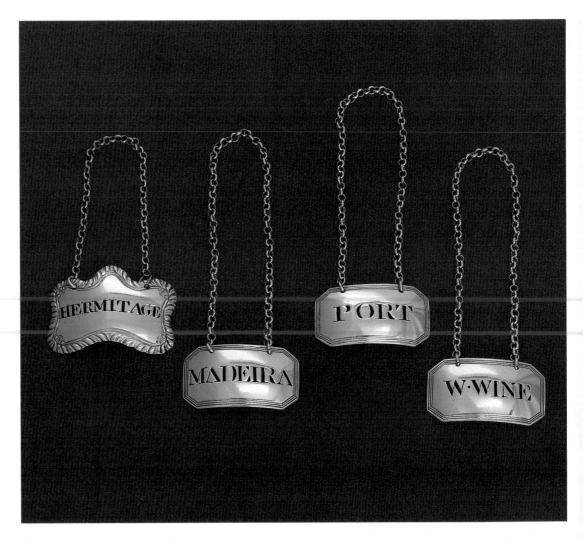

Opposite: (*Pl. 17*)  A variety of wine accessories: a lovely REGENCY GOBLET (1812) by Rebecca Emes and Edward Barnard that recalls earlier forms and GEORGE III WINE LABELS (1792) by Susanna Barker. The cut-glass decanter rests in a silver and wood GEORGE IV WINE COASTER (1823) by Emes and Barnard. The WILLIAM III OVAL TOBACCO BOX (*ca.* 1695) is by Elizabeth Haselwood.

(*Pl. 18*)  *May Day* (*ca.* 1740) by Francis Hayman. In this somewhat romanticized version of milkmaids dancing for their customers on May Day, a porter or chairman carries the maids' headdress or garland of silver objects. Hayman's large canvas (54 × 92 in.) was painted for the supper boxes at Vauxhall Gardens. (Courtesy of the Trustees of the Victoria and Albert Museum)

## 3. Salvers, waiters, and trays

The terms *salver*, *waiter*, and *tray* often cause confusion. Salvers, also called waiters, began as small disks on a central trumpet foot (much like a modern cake stand). They were used by a servant to carry glasses, cups, or goblets, as shown in Marcellus Laroon's intriguing painting of a dinner party (pls. 24 and 25). By the early 18th century, these circular, or occasionally square, stands had descended from their high trumpet pedestals onto three or four low feet which raised their horizontal surface just above a table top. Salvers continued to be used primarily for offering beverages or for protecting the table from heat and moisture. By the mid-18th century they were sometimes employed in sets to hold fruit and delicacies in the center of the dessert table.

This collection includes fine examples of the most popular salver types of the last half of the 18th century. The smaller pair of salvers by Dorothy Sarbitt dating from 1753 (pl. 26) and the larger one marked by her the following year (pl. 21) share certain similarities. With cast shell-and-scroll rims characteristic of rococo fashion, they resemble the "pie-crust" tea tables associated with the Chippendale style of furniture. The larger of these three salvers retains its lovely asymmetrical, rococo armorial engraving (fig. 12).

The small, slightly hexagonal salver marked by Elizabeth Cooke in 1767 (pl. 19) is indicative of the transition from the rococo style to the early neoclassical style influenced by the Adam brothers. The new fashion is seen in the regularity of the repetitive, basket-weave cavetto and the rather heavy gadrooning with its ruffle-like edge. Unfortunately, the original engraving has been erased and replaced with a recently inscribed initial.

Ten years later, in 1777, Louisa Courtauld and George Cowles marked a thoroughly neoclassical salver (pl. 20). The rim of the narrow cavetto is a perfect circle edged with pearling,

46

(*Pl. 19*) GEORGE III SALVER, Elizabeth Cooke, London, 1767. The ruffled, gadrooned rim and simpler lines of this piece herald the emergence of the neoclassical style promoted during the 1760s by Robert and James Adam. (Diameter: 6¾ in.)

(*Pl. 20*) GEORGE III SALVER, Louisa Courtauld and George Cowles, London, *ca.* 1777. The diaper pattern decorating the surface of this salver was designed to disguise scratches resulting from use. (Diameter: 6⅜ in.)

Above: (*Fig. 12*)  Crest from
GEORGE II SALVER by Dorothy
Sarbitt.

Right: (*Pl. 21*)  GEORGE II
SALVER, Dorothy Sarbitt, London,
1754. The especially nice rococo
armorials on this piece have an
asymmetrical foliate cartouche which
encloses the arms of Bischoff,
originally of Basel, Switzerland,
impaling those of an unidentified
party. (Diameter: 11¾ in.)

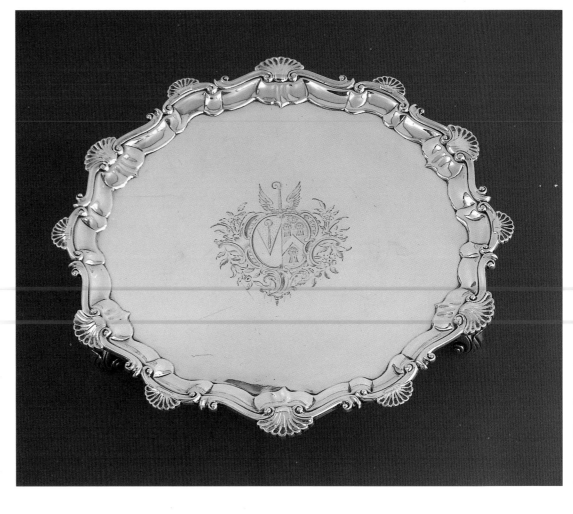

Opposite:
Below left: (*Pl. 23*)  GEORGE III
TRAY, Elizabeth Jones, London,
1795. The sophisticated interplay of
lines and the simple reeded molding
add to the elegance of this piece.
Jones seems to have made trays and
salvers exclusively. (Length: 22¾ in.)

Below right: (*Fig. 14*)  Crest from
GEORGE III TRAY by Elizabeth
Jones.

a decorative motif derived directly from ancient Roman platters excavated in Italy. The center of
the salver has an all-over, loosely engraved pattern resembling quilting. This surface adornment
cleverly disguises the inevitable scratches which accumulate on such pieces from use.

The large salver marked by Hester Bateman in 1779 (pl. 22) is even more characteristic of the
dominant style of the last decades of the 18th century in its restrained simplicity. The narrow
cavetto is outlined with beading which differs from the pearled edge of the Courtauld and
Cowles salver only in scale. The engraved coat of arms, with an oval reserve, pointed shield,
and sparse garlands (fig. 13), is typically neoclassical in its linear symmetry. Engravers of this
period employed the bright-cut technique that removed irregular chips of silver. This resulted
in a scintillating contrast between the engraving and the smoothly planished, "tight skin"
surface of the metal. The arms have been identified as those of Westby impaling Fletcher for
William Westby, Esq., of Thornhill, County Dublin, and his first wife, Mary Fletcher of
Tottenham, whom he married in 1781. The variance in date between the assay date and
Westby's wedding indicates that this item was finished and held in stock, a practice which only
the largest silver firms, such as the Bateman enterprise, could afford, and then only with their
most commonly requested and standard forms. Extremely plain neoclassical silver of this kind,
ornamented only with restrained engraving, was especially popular outside London. Members
of the nobility residing in the capital itself favored silver adorned with embossed husks, swags,
and masks, such as that produced by the famous Courtauld family of silversmiths (see pl. 37).

Trays, defined as large, oval (or later rectangular) servers with two handles, were not
introduced until the end of the 18th century. The 1795 tray by Elizabeth Jones in this collection

Left: (*Pl. 22*)  GEORGE III
CIRCULAR SALVER, Hester Bateman,
London, 1779. To be successful, an
elegantly simple salver such as this
must have perfect proportions, a fine
surface finish, and delicate, deliberate
engraving. The arms on this salver
are Westby impaling Fletcher for
William Westby, Esq., of Thornhill,
County Dublin, and his first wife,
Mary Fletcher, daughter of George
Fletcher, Esq., of Tottenham. Their
marriage took place on April 18,
1781. (Diameter: $12\frac{7}{8}$ in.)

Above: (*Fig. 13*)  Crest from
GEORGE III CIRCULAR SALVER by
Hester Bateman.

Right: (*Pl. 24*) and detail below (*Pl. 25*) *A Dinner Party* by Marcellus Laroon the Younger (1679–1774). At this lavish affair a variety of silver salvers and trays are employed to carry drinks and desserts to the table and to hold fruit. (By gracious permission of Her Majesty Queen Elizabeth II)

with its simple reeded edge is an excellent example of the early tray form (pl. 23). Jones is known to have specialized in salvers and trays, which by this period could be made from pre-rolled sheet silver with relative ease. Unfortunately, the large, engraved armorial is a later, 19th-century addition. Although quite handsome, its more emphatic style differs from the tray itself (fig. 14).

## 4. Tea and coffee services

Much has been written about the history of tea and its tremendous impact on Western commerce, economics, politics, arts, and crafts. Surprisingly less has been recorded about the enormous social changes caused by the advent of tea. Except in the case of royalty and courtesans, social life prior to the 18th century was dominated by men. Even well into the 19th century, celebratory state banquets were attended exclusively by men, while women remained observers, relegated to balconies or anterooms. Gentlemen took pride in their extensive wine cellars and their skill at mixing a potent punch. Ladies, however, did not imbibe such spirits. For more than a century after the introduction of tea into England at the end of the 17th century, tea was exorbitantly expensive—far too precious to be entrusted to a mere servant for brewing! Although gentlemen undertook the making of punch and often even the decanting of wine, it was the lady of the house who took the responsibility for preparing and serving tea. Thus it was

*(Pl. 26)* PAIR OF GEORGE II SALVERS, Dorothy Sarbitt, London, 1753. Salvers developed as a polite way to offer a beverage. They also were used as an attractive means of presenting fruit on a dessert table. Raised on small feet, they protected the wood and table covering from moisture. (Diameter of each: $7\frac{1}{2}$ in.)

51

tea, with its connotations of the exotic and rare, that opened the door for women's greater participation in social life.

Numerous 18th-century depictions of both public and private gatherings, such as William Hogarth's painting *Assembly at Wanstead House* from 1728–31 (pl. 27), include a woman presiding over the teapot. In fact, by the 19th century, tea had become so much a part of the female domain that it came to be associated with such "womanly" attributes as warmth and comfort. Artists of the late 19th century, like Mary Cassatt, used the sharing of tea to symbolize female companionship (pl. 29). Later, at the turn of the 20th century, tea services themselves became allusions to women's grace and beauty, just as the hand mirror previously had been the artistic emblem of Venus.

In a collection of silver marked by women, it is hardly surprising to find a large number of pieces designed for the service of tea or to note that many of them are exquisitely beautiful and

well made. When tea first arrived from China, the delicately exotic cups and pots of porcelain, which the Chinese had invented, were quickly adopted and became at least as desirable as the tea leaves themselves. When other objects, such as tea containers, cake stands, and cream vessels, were needed for the tea table, the English adapted objects already in use. They frequently employed silver in their manufacture, a fine material which matched the rarity and value of the Chinese porcelain and the tea.

Small silver bottles and boxes were borrowed from the well-appointed dressing table, such as that represented in Johann Zoffany's lavish portrait of Queen Charlotte (pl. 28), to serve as containers for the dried tea leaves. For security, these silver containers, usually purchased in pairs along with a matching sugar box, were fitted into lacquered or leather-covered cases that could be locked. A tea chest containing tea caddies is depicted at the corner of the carpet in Joseph van Aken's *An English Family at Tea*, dating from about 1720 (pls. 34 and 35). The

*(Pl. 28) Queen Charlotte at her Dressing Table* (1764) by Johann Zoffany (1733–1810). The gilt or silver objects on elegant dressing tables influenced the form of early boxes and bottles used for tea leaves. (By gracious permission of Her Majesty Queen Elizabeth II)

(Pl. 29) *Five O'Clock Tea* (1880) by Mary Stevenson Cassatt (1844–1926). The tea service is very similar to one in the museum's collection marked by Ann, Peter, and William Bateman. (Courtesy of the Museum of Fine Arts, Boston—M. Theresa B. Hopkins Fund)

Opposite: (Pl. 30) A tea ensemble sitting on a GEORGE III CIRCULAR SALVER (1779) by Hester Bateman. The GEORGE III TEA SET (1800) is by Ann, Peter, and William Bateman and the GEORGE III CAST SUGAR TONGS (late 18th/early 19th century) by Hester Bateman.

Malaysian word *kati*, designating a unit of measurement almost equivalent to a British pound, was soon adapted to *caddy* as the name of the tea container itself. Understandably, caddies and other tea equipment were often made in the rococo chinoiserie style. Chinoiserie, the decorative expression of the West's fantasies about the Orient, combined Chinese, Japanese, Indian, and even Turkish motifs with fashionable occidental shapes and designs. The imaginary oriental world of chinoiserie in turn inspired Chinese copies for European trade, which simply reinforced the West's confusion about the Orient and its aesthetic values.

The pair of tea caddies marked by Elizabeth Godfrey in 1755 (pls. 32 and 33) are prime examples of chinoiserie at its most exuberant. The *bombé* form of the boxes and low, scroll bracket feet are derived from French rococo furniture in the Louis XV style. The abundant decoration on the caddies incorporates rococo scrolls, shells, flowers, and miniature chinoiserie scenes. It is executed in the embossed, or *repoussé*, technique, by which the design is tapped from the interior of the finished piece and then refined on the outside with chasing. Whenever possible, tea was offered in two varieties—usually black and green—and could also be blended according to individual preference.

Above: (*Pl. 31*) and detail of crest right (*Fig. 15*)  GEORGE II TEA CADDY, Elizabeth Godfrey, London, 1758. With its ornate repoussé shells and scrolls, this caddy is characteristically French rococo in style. Such decoration requires a relatively thin gauge of silver, but ultimately strengthens the walls of the piece, which would be subject to dents if left smooth. (Height: 5⅜ in.)

A third tea caddy by Elizabeth Godfrey was marked in 1758, three years later than the chinoiserie pair (pl. 31). It is similar to the earlier caddies in form and style but lacks the orientalizing details, being more French rococo in appearance (fig. 15). These three charming boxes were standard, if somewhat lavish, pieces from a sophisticated silver shop, and demon-strate the prevalence of the French influence on English silver in the mid-18th century. Although labor intensive, the repoussé technique was fairly inexpensive to produce as it required the use of a relatively thin gauge of silver. The latest fashion could, therefore, be copied for a reasonable price.

Vase-form caddies, such as those marked by Louisa Courtauld and Samuel Courtauld I in 1766 (pl. 37), were more difficult to make and are, therefore, rarer. Similar containers also were designed for condiments and sugar. The reason for Louisa Courtauld's success and high standing in the craft of silversmithing is evident from these sophisticated caddies, designed in the highly fashionable neoclassical style popularized by Robert and James Adam. In striking contrast to the French rococo of the previous decade, the early neoclassical style—rational, formal, and restrained—was based on ancient Roman models. The appeal of neoclassical silver lay in its simple elegance, not in its ornamentation. In fact, the embossed drapery swags and masks found on these refined caddies were omitted on less expensive silver and on Sheffield plate, where repoussé work was quite likely to cause the thin silver-plated surface to crack or flake.

Above: (*Pl. 32*) and detail left (*Pl. 33*) PAIR OF GEORGE II TEA CADDIES, Elizabeth Godfrey, London, 1755. These are excellent examples of English rococo silver in the chinoiserie manner. The front and back panels, which are decorated with oriental scenes incorporating tea planters and pickers, are highly appropriate for containers created to hold a Chinese luxury item. Godfrey's Huguenot ancestry is evident in the French styling of these works. (Height of each: approx. $5\frac{1}{2}$ in.)

Above: (Pl. 34) and detail right (Pl. 35)   *An English Family at Tea* (*ca. 1720*) by Joseph van Aken (1709–49). The servant holds a round kettle that may be warmed on the lamp stand to the right. A lockable box for two tea caddies rests at the edge of the carpet. (Courtesy of the Tate Gallery, London)

Opposite: (Pl. 36)   Shown here are Magdalen Feline's GEORGE II KETTLE ON LAMP STAND (1756) and Dinah Gamon's GEORGE II CREAMER (1743). The French rococo GEORGE II TEA CADDY (1758) is by Elizabeth Godfrey. The GEORGE III TEA CADDY SPOON (1797) is by Elizabeth Morley. The Sarah Blake TEASPOONS (1812) are from the Regency period.

On less expensive wares, such as those exported to America, the sculpted bands of leaves and gadrooning seen on these caddies were replaced by more restrained flat chasing or engraving. Roman-style tea caddies were made as many as forty years later by such master silversmiths as Paul Storr, demonstrating the extraordinarily long life of this classic form.

The oval, box-form caddy marked by Ann Robertson in 1802 is made in one of the most popular shapes of the late 18th century, and represents a quite different manifestation of the neoclassical style (pl. 41). Circular or oval straight-sided caddies could be produced easily and inexpensively from sheets of mechanically rolled silver, which were simply cut and seamed. The gently domed cover was a refinement introduced after the 1780s. The restriction of the engraved borders to carefully controlled ribbons, instead of loose swags or irregular bands, and the circular reserve date this caddy late in the neoclassical period, just prior to the emergence of the heavier, more horizontal Regency and French Empire styles. By the late 18th century, the middle class for which this simple, standard caddy was intended had abandoned the attempt to serve two types of tea. Green or "China" tea continued to be the choice of the privileged classes, and the cheaper, black or "India" tea the preference of the middle and lower classes. The custom of providing a case with two caddies began to die out, but individual caddies still were locked. If the Courtauld caddies represent the products made by the most fashionable London silversmiths for an élite clientele, this Robertson caddy made in Newcastle upon Tyne exemplifies the attractive, competent, simplified work of provincial silversmiths whose clients came from the growing middle class.

Matching tea or coffee services consisting of several pieces did not come into general use until at least 1785. Prior to that date, services were accumulated gradually over an extended period and included pieces of imported china, English ceramics, and silver. Often the first item of silver hollow ware acquired for the tea table was a cream pitcher, as shown by William Hogarth's charming painting of the Strode family at tea, dating from approximately 1738 (pls. 38 and 39). Apparently the English did not begin diluting their tea with cream, offered by the drop, before the reign of Queen Anne (1702–14), and tea sets did not necessarily include a cream pot until the mid-18th century. As the middle class began to drink more tea in the 19th century, milk generally replaced cream. Little jugs and cream boats were probably first borrowed from the dessert table, where they had held sweet cream, custard, or syrupy sauces. The baluster form of the Dinah Gamon cream pot assayed in 1743 (pl. 40) was developed during the 1730s. The flat scroll and floral chasing is an early example of the rococo style. This charming piece undoubtedly added luster and fashion to a table arranged with a Chinese-export porcelain teapot and cups.

While the Gamon cream pitcher dates from the very beginning of the rococo style, the cream pot produced by Anne Smith and Nathaniel Appleton in 1773 marks the end of the period (pl. 43). The pot itself is an inverted pyriform, or pear shape, that lends a typically rococo sense of imbalance. In fact, like many similar, late-rococo cream pots, the thin gauge and tall pedestal of this piece make it so unstable that a lump of base metal had to be added to the foot. The floral, raised chasing, the double scroll handle, and the scalloped edge of the everted lip are characteristic features of rococo. The chased ruffle gadrooning on the foot is typical of the 1770s. This sort of pretty but somewhat insubstantial piece was produced in quantity and widely retailed by jewelers, fancy-goods dealers, "toymen" who specialized in small luxuries, and even stationers. It might well have been the only piece of silver, apart from spoons, in a successful tradesman's home.

Opposite: (Pl. 37)  PAIR OF GEORGE III TEA CADDIES, Louisa Courtauld and Samuel Courtauld I, London, 1766. Demonstrating the great elegance and sophistication characteristic of the neoclassical style, these caddies are extremely advanced and fashionable for the mid-1760s. (Height of each: 7⅜ in.)

Above: (*Pl. 38*) and detail right (*Pl. 39*) *The Strode Family* (*ca.* 1738) by William Hogarth (1697–1764). William Strode (middle) and his mother, Lady Ann Strode, entertain Dr. Arthur Smith to tea. Their tea service includes a silver cream jug, a silver "skittle-ball" kettle, and a silver salver. (Courtesy of the Tate Gallery, London; Photo John Webb)

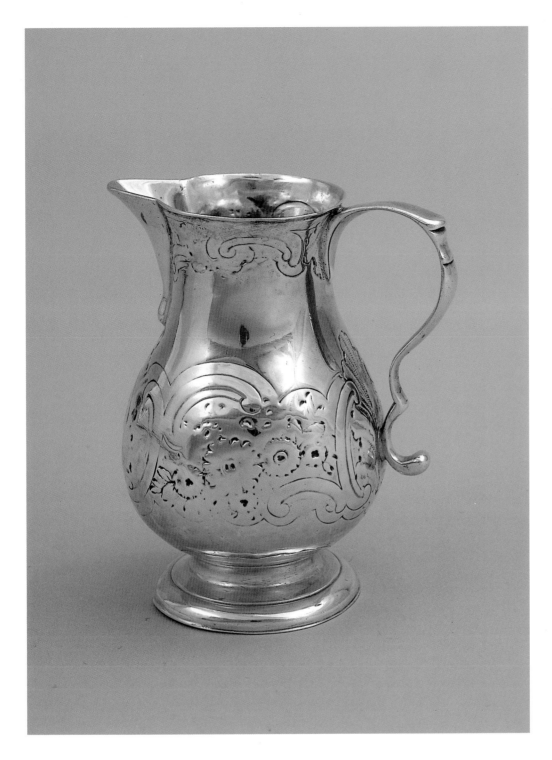

(*Pl. 40*)  GEORGE II CREAMER,
Dinah Gamon, London, 1743.
Dating from the period which
preceded the demand for matching
tea sets, this creamer probably
accompanied a Chinese export
porcelain teapot and cups. Its
decoration is a fine example of flat
chasing in the rococo style. The tiny
size reminds us that the cream it held
was dispensed by the drop. (Height:
$3\frac{1}{8}$ in.)

By 1790 the restless ornamentation and curves of the Smith and Appleton cream pot were refined into a tall, elegant helmet form. Around 1800 a flat base was substituted for the pedestal and plinth, creating the jug forming part of a three-piece set which was marked in 1800 by Ann, Peter, and William Bateman (see pl. 53), and the similar jug marked by Ann and Peter Bateman in 1804 (pl. 44). As milk began to replace cream in tea, larger vessels came to be made, as the Dorothy Langlands tea set of 1809–12 reveals (see pl. 56).

In the 17th century the sugar used to enhance wine had been kept in small, robust, casket-shaped boxes derived from dressing-table jewel cases. As sugar began to be taken with tea, these were considered too clumsy for the tea table, and a variety of porcelain or silver boxes and

(*Pl. 41*) GEORGE III TEA CADDY, Ann Robertson, Newcastle upon Tyne, 1802. This is an example of the pretty neoclassical silver found in provincial centers like Newcastle. The attractive, ribbon-like decorative motif became fashionable around 1800. Tea was still considered extremely valuable when this caddy was made, necessitating the lock on the front. (Height: 6 in.)

covered bowls were adopted. During the neoclassical period, sugar containers took on other forms, such as covered, vase-shaped containers like the tea caddies discussed earlier or open, swing-handled basket shapes. One of the most charming, yet least expensive, methods of decorating silver during the neoclassical period was the *ajouré*, or piercing, technique. A fine example is the 1777 Hester Bateman sugar basket, shown to advantage by a Bristol blue-glass liner (pl. 42 and fig. 16). At first, piercing was laboriously accomplished with watchmakers' saws, but the introduction of stamping machines soon reduced time and labor and also produced more even holes. The use of thin, machine-rolled sheets of silver strengthened by machine-drawn beaded wire and decorated with machine-pierced designs resulted in light wares which could be afforded by a much wider market. Such silver was especially suitable for export because shipping costs were often calculated by weight.

(*Pl. 42*)　George III glass-lined
sugar basket, Hester Bateman,
London, 1777. The blue-glass liner
provides a charming contrast to the
pierced foliate borders, trellis work,
and engraved swags of the silver.
(Height: $5\frac{1}{4}$ in.)

(*Fig. 16*)　Detail of ajouré and
engraving on the George III
glass-lined sugar basket by
Hester Bateman.

(*Pl. 43*)  GEORGE III CREAM JUG,
Anne Smith and Nathaniel
Appleton, London, 1773. The
cusped edge, inverted pear-shaped
body, and floral chasing of this piece
are rococo in style, but there is
evidence of the dawning of
neoclassicism in the pedestal base and
gadrooned edge. The Smith and
Appleton mark has been found only
on cream jugs and salt cellars.
(Height: 4 in.)

(*Pl. 44*) GEORGE III CREAMER, Ann Bateman and Peter Bateman, London, 1804. Around 1800 a flat base was substituted for the earlier pedestal and plinth form used for some cream jugs. (Height: $5\frac{1}{2}$ in.)

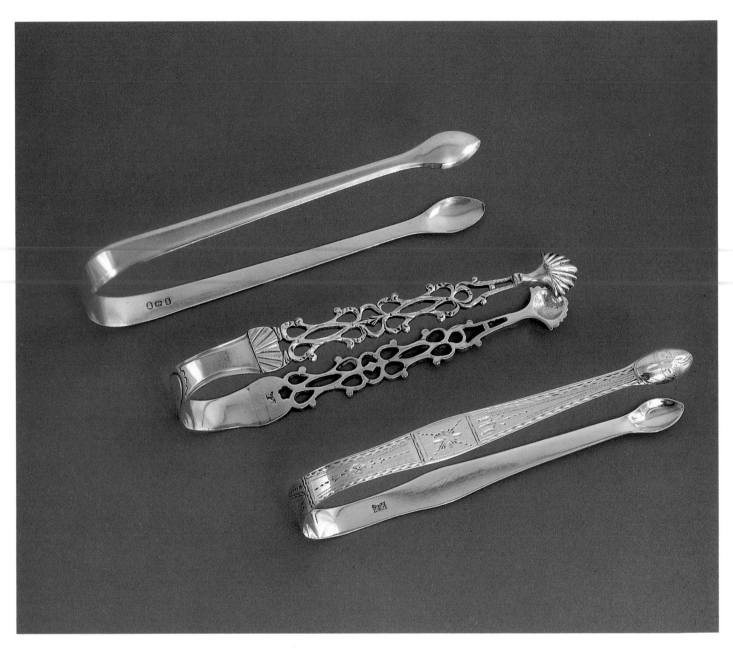

(Pl. 45) GEORGE III PLAIN SUGAR TONGS (top), Ann, Peter, and William Bateman, London, 1804; GEORGE III CAST SUGAR TONGS (middle), Hester Bateman, London, late 18th/early 19th century; GEORGE III BRIGHT-CUT SUGAR TONGS (bottom), Hester Bateman, London, late 18th/early 19th century. The more elaborate cast and pierced tongs predate the simpler form. (Length: approx. 5¾ in.)

Opposite: (Pl. 46) GEORGE III SUGAR BASKET, Hester Bateman, London, 1786. (Length: 7¾ in.)

A second sugar basket, of 1786, also marked by Hester Bateman, is even more appealing with its oval boat shape, graceful pedestal, and delicate bright-cut engraving (pl. 46). Although not produced in great quantity in London, these sugar baskets were copied in such distant locations as Dublin, Ireland, and Baltimore, Maryland.

It is appropriate that the three sugar tongs in this collection (pl. 45) are all marked by members of the Bateman family because such tongs would have been used to serve lump sugar from the two Hester Bateman baskets just discussed. The earliest sugar-serving utensils looked like miniature fire tongs. Scissor-like sugar nips were made for several decades in the mid-18th century. They were followed in the 1770s by cast, open-work arms soldered to a tempered U-shaped spring. After 1780 tongs were made by bending and tempering a long strip of silver. Sugar tongs, which did not necessarily match tea and coffee services of other flatware, made affordable gifts.

(*Pl. 47*)  *A Family at Tea* (*ca. 1725*) by an unknown English artist. The shapes of the covered sugar bowl and the tea caddies were borrowed from dressing table items such as those in pl. 28. (Courtesy of the Trustees of the Victoria and Albert Museum, London)

Opposite: (*Pl. 48*)  GEORGE II LAMP STAND, Magdalen Feline, London, 1753. This stand probably was used for a kettle. Its four double-scroll supports rest on cast, shell feet. (Height: 3¾ in.)

A very fine tea kettle of 1756, marked by Magdalen Feline, harks back to earlier stages in the development of tea equipment (pl. 50). Originally tea was brewed and served in minuscule quantities. There are accounts of individual guests consuming a dozen cups of tea at one sitting, for 18th-century cups often held as little as one or two fluid ounces. Teapots were particularly small in the early years of the century; therefore, hot water was needed close at hand to dilute the brewed tea and to make fresh pots of tea. Kettles with swing handles and fitted lamp stands were popular but were usually made of copper or brass. A silver kettle and stand may be seen in several of the paintings mentioned earlier, particularly van Aken's *An English Family at Tea* (pls. 34 and 35). The small capacity of the Magdalen Feline kettle highlights the expensiveness of silver and the value placed on tea. The high quality of this piece is evident in its bold form and substantial weight, as well as in the fine detailing of the cast lamp stand (fig. 18) and engraved rococo armorial. The heat generated by the boiling water required the silversmith to incorporate a wooden finial on the cover and wrap raffia around the handle for insulation.

Right: (*Pl. 49*)  GEORGE III
TEAPOT, Alice Burrows and George
Burrows II, London, 1803. The
drum shape, flat cover, and conical
spout demonstrate design changes
developed by silversmiths which took
advantage of the availability of
machine-rolled sheet silver. The flush
hinge is a fine example of the art of
silversmithing. (Height: $5\frac{1}{8}$ in.)
GEORGE III TEAPOT STAND,
Hannah Northcote, London, 1809.
The reeded edge and engraved band
of this teapot stand are typical of the
style that followed stands with
beading and claw feet. (Length:
$6\frac{3}{8}$ in.)

Below right: (*Fig. 17*)  Detail of
bright-cut engraving on GEORGE III
TEAPOT by Alice Burrows and
George Burrows II.

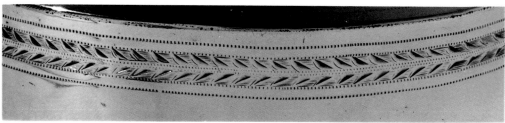

Opposite: (*Pl. 50*) and detail of stand
below (*Fig. 18*)  GEORGE II
KETTLE ON LAMP STAND, Magdalen
Feline, London, 1756. Sometimes
called a "skittle-ball" kettle after the
popular game of skittles, this piece
has a massive presence although it is
relatively small. The stand is
whimsically decorated with feathers
and birds' heads. The engraved coat
of arms is the only rococo feature of
this highly functional work. (Height
on stand: $9\frac{1}{2}$ in.)

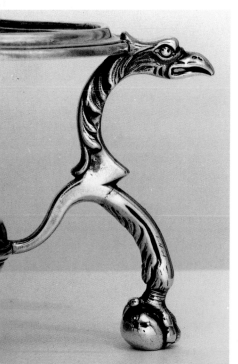

The bulbous form of such kettles suited the rococo style but did not lend itself to the neoclassical taste for attenuation. The kettle form, therefore, was supplanted by the urn. Urns either had a spirit lamp in the pedestal or contained an interior sleeve which held a rod of hot iron.

The urn was the archetypal shape of the neoclassical style and was used for everything from heating stoves to jewelry. Coffee pots almost invariably took the form of a classical urn, and more sophisticated teapots also were designed in the shape of an urn. The availability of rolled sheet silver, however, led to the creation of a simplified form of silver teapot which was easier to manufacture.

The simplest neoclassical teapots were made of a long rectangle of sheet silver soldered into a drum or oval shape. A disk of thin silver was then soldered on to form the bottom, and another piece was used for the hinged cover. An elongated cone formed the spout, and two small cylinders created sockets into which the wooden, C-scroll handle was pinned. Bright-cut engraving, which could be produced quickly and easily (fig. 17), provided the decoration on the 1803 pot by Alice and George Burrows, which epitomizes this type of teapot (pl. 49). The drum-shaped pot was common between about 1760 and 1785, so the 1803 assay date on the Burrows pot suggests that it was made to match or replace a piece from an earlier service.

(*Pl. 51*)  GEORGE III TEAPOT STAND, Elizabeth Jones, London, 1783. This oval stand with a nicely beaded border and claw feet originally was intended to protect table tops from the moisture and heat of a drum-shaped teapot. Later it may well have been used to receive calling cards or pass delicacies. (Length: 6¼ in.)

Opposite: (*Pl. 52*)  GEORGE III TEAPOT ON STAND, Hester Bateman, London, 1788. The cut-cornered, or "four-square," teapot is a pleasing refinement of the earlier rectangular shape. It is unusual that the teapot and stand have remained together. (Height on stand: 7¼ in.)

Drum-shaped teapots were originally provided with stands to protect the table tops. The beaded edge of the Elizabeth Jones teapot stand dated 1783 (pl. 51) precedes the reeded edge and ribbon-like engraved border of the Hannah Northcote example of 1809 (pl. 49). When calling cards became the rage in the last half of the 19th century, many teapot stands were pressed into service as small salvers or card receivers and became separated from their teapots. It is fortunate that the cut-cornered, rectangular stand survives with the earliest teapot in the collection, hallmarked by Hester Bateman in 1788, for it reveals the added elegance achieved by placing teapots on stands (pl. 52). The rectangle form was one of several possible variants for drum-shaped teapots. Other variations in shape included oval, regularly or irregularly fluted, and serpentine. The covers of these unusual teapot forms were frequently domed. The angles created by fluting or shaping also added structural strength to the thinly rolled, untempered silver from which these teapots were made.

A new, bolder style is evident in the curving sides, swan-neck spout, concave shoulders, and reeded edges of the teapot and matching pieces produced by Ann, Peter, and William Bateman in 1800 (pl. 53). Only a decade later an entirely different style in silver tea wares emerged, incorporating more complex profiles, chased lobing around the lower bodies, repetitive engraved or machined ornamentation, and ball feet. The strongly horizontal sweep of the 1816 teapot by Alice Burrows (pl. 57) and the tea set marked by Dorothy Langlands around 1810 (pl. 56) is diametrically opposed to the verticality of the earlier neoclassical style. The Langlands set is also an interesting example of a tea service that appears at first to match.

(*Pl. 53*)  GEORGE III TEA SET, Ann Bateman, Peter Bateman, and William Bateman, London, 1800. This elegantly simple type of silver was easily produced and inexpensive enough to be exported. As a result, it was influential in America; almost identical pieces were made by Boston, New York, and Philadelphia silversmiths. (Sugar bowl height: $4\frac{3}{4}$ in.; Teapot height: 7 in.; Creamer height: 4 in.)

Overleaf left: (*Pl. 54*)  GEORGE II COFFEE POT, Elizabeth Godfrey, London, 1743. Coffee and tea were not served at the same time, and, consequently, the shapes of their respective containers developed in very different directions. This is a good example of the 18th-century coffee pot form. (Height: $6\frac{7}{8}$ in.)

Overleaf right: (*Pl. 55*)  GEORGE III COFFEE POT, attributed to Hester Bateman, London, 1780. A baluster form on a spreading foot, with a swan-neck spout and wooden scroll handle. (Height: $12\frac{1}{4}$ in.)

Top: (*Fig. 19*)   Detail of teapot from
GEORGE III TEA SET by Dorothy
Langlands.

Above: (*Fig. 20*)   Detail of creamer
from GEORGE III TEA SET by
Dorothy Langlands.

Right: (*Fig. 21*)   Detail of sugar
bowl from GEORGE III TEA SET by
Dorothy Langlands.

A closer look at the engraving and other decorative details (figs. 19, 20, and 21), however, reveals that each piece was made by a different artisan. The creamer is probably by Urquhart and Hart.

Sugar bowls made in Britain and Ireland after 1800 were not covered, perhaps as a development of the sugar basket form. By contrast, 19th-century American sugar bowls invariably had loose covers, even when the bowl was shaped like the English version. While most tea-service pieces were made to match and sold as an ensemble by 1800, large sugar bowls with matching creamers were sometimes sold separately to be used with fruit for dessert or with a ceramic teapot. Thus it is possible that there was never a silver teapot to match the Ann Robertson sugar bowl and cream jug from 1810 (pl. 58). The lobing on the lower half of these pieces is given prominence by the unusual panels of matting that emphasize the sculptural and textural properties of the design.

Coffee and tea were never served at the same time during the 18th century. In fact, sets of china cups were often made in groups of a dozen tea cups, a dozen coffee cups, and a dozen saucers to be used with either cups as appropriate. Coffee pots, derived from the early, cylindrical lighthouse form, have continued, with almost no exceptions, to be taller and more vertical than teapots. The small coffee pot marked by Elizabeth Godfrey in 1743 is a fine example of a type popular during most of the 18th century (pl. 54). The low dome of the cover and conical, rather than pear-shaped, body are characteristics of the early rococo style. The somewhat oversized spout and handle sockets are reminders that molds for such parts were expensive and a variety of sizes was not always available. The large handle and spout are sensitively balanced by the skillfully engraved rococo armorial.

(Pl. 56)   GEORGE III TEA SET, Dorothy Langlands, Newcastle upon Tyne, 1809–12. Although apparently a matching set, careful examination of the marks, details, and engraving on these pieces reveals that they were made by different artisans. In fact, the creamer probably was made by Urquhart and Hart, while the teapot and sugar bowl are the work of Langlands. During this period matching tea sets were still a novelty among the middle class. (Creamer height: $3\frac{1}{2}$ in.; Teapot height: $6\frac{1}{2}$ in.; Sugar bowl height: $4\frac{1}{4}$ in.)

(*Pl. 57*)  REGENCY TEAPOT, Alice Burrows and George Burrows II, London, 1816. The directional lobing joins in a central heart shape on the side of the teapot—a pretty refinement. (Height: $5\frac{1}{8}$ in.)

(*Pl. 58*)  GEORGE III CREAMER AND SUGAR BOWL, Ann Robertson, Newcastle upon Tyne, *ca.* 1810. The matted panels between the chased lobes on the lower body of these pieces are quite unusual. (Creamer height: $4\frac{3}{8}$ in.; Sugar bowl height: $4\frac{7}{8}$ in.)

## 5. Candlesticks

Casting pieces in a mold requires a great deal of metal and results in a very heavy object that does not have the tensile strength of silver which has been hammered and annealed. Generally, only part of the object is cast. Casting is very suitable, although expensive, for making candlesticks, however. Candlesticks that are not cast, but rather formed of thin pieces of shaped silver, must be filled and weighted with pitch or plaster of Paris. Both candlesticks in the pair marked by Mary Gould in 1747 (pl. 60) were cast in three parts: one piece for the base (fig. 22) and two pieces soldered vertically for the stem and nozzle. The casting and finishing of such items were relatively easy and inexpensive, but the amount of silver used made candlesticks costly, and the styles of cast candlesticks changed rather slowly. Only the very rich had the means with which to purchase cast candlesticks.

Unusually, the Gould pair is marked with her husband's initials. They are a standard design made by silversmiths who specialized in candlesticks and by artisans who offered more varied wares. Candlesticks of this type were used on card tables, the corners of which sometimes were shaped to hold them, as well as on dining and dressing tables. They also provided general

*(Pl. 59)* This delightful still life of a tea table by an anonymous English artist, which dates from 1770, depicts the variety of interesting objects that were related to the service of tea at that time. An urn-shaped hot water heater is used to fill a porcelain teapot. Silver sugar nippers protrude from a sugar vase, the cover of which rests on the tea tray. The rococo candlesticks attest to the fact that candles were a constant presence in 18th-century homes, used to provide illumination at teas, dinners, and many other social activities. (Courtesy of the Trustees of the Victoria and Albert Museum)

Right: (*Pl. 60*) and detail of base below (*Fig. 22*) PAIR OF GEORGE II SILVER-GILT CANDLESTICKS, Mary Gould, London, 1747. These candlesticks use a shell motif, the fashionable ornamentation of the period, to great advantage. Mary Gould was almost exclusively a candlestick maker. She did not register a mark herself but used her husband's mark, *IG*. (Height of each: 8 in.)

lighting at a period when two or three candles were considered sufficient illumination. This pair may not have been gilded originally; the gilding now visible was produced by the relatively modern electroplating process.

## 6. Dinner services

The dining habits of the 18th and 19th centuries were quite different from those today and required different types of silverware. Dinner was served in the middle of the day and divided the waking hours into the morning and evening. The meal consisted of at least two or three

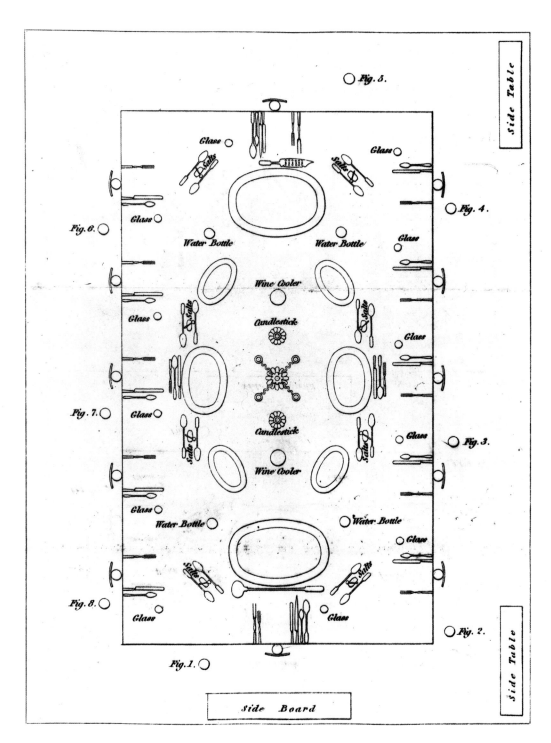

Inside the diagram:

Side Table

Fig. 5.

Glass — Glass

Salts — Salts

Fig. 6.  Glass

Water Bottle — Water Bottle

Glass

Wine Cooler

Fig. 4.

Salts — Salts

Glass

Candlestick

Glass

Fig. 7.  Glass

Salts — Salts

Candlestick

Glass  Fig. 3.

Wine Cooler

Glass

Water Bottle — Water Bottle  Glass

Fig. 8.  Glass

Salts — Salts

Fig. 2.

Glass — Glass

Fig. 1.

Side Table

Side Board

(*Fig. 23*)   *Dinner Table Set Out for Twelve Persons With Eight Attendants* from *The Footman's Directory* 5th ed. (1825) by Thomas Cosnett. (Courtesy of The Winterthur Library—Printed Book and Periodical Collection)

courses, each composed of several dozen dishes, which were laid out symmetrically and virtually covered the table top. Diagrams illustrating the proper way to lay a table (fig. 23) have been published for several centuries in etiquette books, such as Thomas Cosnett's *The Footman's Directory* of 1825. Because the dinner service was arranged symmetrically, almost all serving dishes were produced in pairs or even-numbered sets. One of the few documented exceptions to this rule was the dish cross which occupied the center of the table, as illustrated in Cosnett's diagram. The drawing also shows trencher salts, an early type of salt cellar without feet, between paired tablespoons at alternate place settings and a soup ladle at one end and a fish

(*Pl. 61*)  Pair of George I
trencher salts, Mary Rood,
London, 1723. Trenchers were
individual slabs of hard bread or
wood that served as personal plates.
Trencher salts, which developed as
stylish status symbols, were placed
next to each individual trencher or
between every other guest. (Height of
each: 1 in.)

slice at the other, all pieces represented in the collection. Although extremely wealthy families owned sets comprising dozens of silver plates and dishes along with soup tureens and other covered dishes, such services were beyond the reach of all but the noble class. Plates and flat dishes offer the silversmith limited opportunities for stylistic or decorative invention and are prone to damage. Sets of silver dining equipment, therefore, were rare, and "mixing and matching" was the order of the day.

Prior to refrigerators, meat was preserved either by drying, a process which resulted in such bland food that highly flavored spices and condiments were needed, or by smoking or salting, which produced such highly seasoned foodstuffs that neutralizing sauces were required. The most interesting and varied silver dinnerware thus falls into the category of containers for seasonings. Certainly the most common condiment containers made of English silver were salt cellars. The former importance of salt is demonstrated by the medieval custom of indicating the relative status of diners by their position at the table in relation to a large, ceremonial salt container. Individual salt dishes became common in the 17th century, although few survive before the early 18th century. It is appropriate that a pair of rectangular trencher salts carrying the date letter for 1723 are among the earliest silver in the collection (pl. 61). The silver of this pair marked by Mary Rood is quite thin and has worn through in some places. The pleasing, cut-cornered style was termed "four square" during the Queen Anne and early Georgian years.

Salt is silver's worst enemy. When combined with moisture, salt eats into the surface of silver, creating unsightly and irreversible black pits. This problem can be avoided by protecting the surface of the silver with a gilded coating or a glass liner. The excellent condition of the Anne Tanqueray circular salts (pl. 62) indicates that they have always been gilded, although the present surface is, in fact, not original. The complex profile and simple massing of these salts, which date from 1732, give them an attractive monumentality.

(*Pl. 62*) Pair of George II silver-gilt salt cellars, Anne Tanqueray, London, 1732. Tanqueray was a member of one of the great Huguenot silversmith families. The design of these cellars is clean-cut and simple, reminiscent of the Queen Anne style. They were formerly in the Patino Collection. (Diameter of each: 3½ in.)

(*Pl. 63*) Set of four George III salt cellars, Anne Smith and Nathaniel Appleton, London, 1782. The everted rim with ruffled gadrooning on these pieces was quite fashionable in the 1780s. Originally, the salt cellars were probably equipped with glass interiors to prevent the salt from damaging the surface of the silver. (Diameter of each: 3 in.)

Above: (*Pl. 64*) and detail opposite (*Pl. 65*) *Captain Lord George Graham in his Cabin* (*ca.* 1745) by William Hogarth (1697–1764). In the days when ships acted as floating embassies, it was mandatory that ships' captains dine in the highest style. Hogarth depicts Lord Graham using silver plates and fashionable silver cutlery. He is also being served from a silver salver. The fact that Lord Graham is not in uniform, dates the painting to before 1748, when the Royal Navy introduced uniforms. (Courtesy of The National Maritime Museum, London)

By far the most common form of 18th-century salt cellar is the compressed hemisphere on three scroll feet. The earliest of this type date from the 1730s, and, while they went out of fashion during the neoclassical period, they were quickly revived in the 19th century. The everted rim and ruffled gadrooning of the four salts marked by Anne Smith and Nathaniel Appleton are characteristic of the 1780s style (pl. 63). They show evidence of salt disease on the inside and probably were fitted originally with clear-glass liners that had matching gadrooned rims. Anne Smith is known to have made only salt cellars and small cream pots.

Mustard was an extremely popular 18th-century condiment. Served in dry, powdered form from tall casters, it was mixed with vinegar on the rim of the plate. It is thought that the flat flange on plates evolved for the purpose of mixing mustard. In William Hogarth's painting *Captain Lord George Graham in his Cabin* (pls. 64 and 65) of *ca.* 1745, for instance, we see silver plates with wide rims on which condiments could be mixed. There are also silver serving dishes, fashionable silver forks very like the one in this collection marked by Mary and Eliza Sumner (see pl. 96), and a silver cup covered by a starched napkin.

Pre-mixed mustard began to be offered in little pots resembling miniature tankards in the mid-18th century. Since mustard stains silver, mustard pots, like salt cellars, need to be gilded or lined. Bristol blue-glass liners enhanced the effect of fanciful neoclassical piercing such as that found on the exquisite oval mustard pot by Hester Bateman (pl. 66). The domed cover is quite advanced for the 1778 assay date of this piece. This sort of attractive, thin-gauge silver sold in quantity and made the Bateman firm a great commercial success.

The charming George II saucepan or brandy warmer by Ann Craig and John Neville (pl. 67) falls under the general category of a condiment container, because warmed brandy tended to be used as a sauce rather than as a beverage. Our ancestors seem to have been just as delighted, if not more so, by blue flames dancing on a joint of meat or a dark pudding. The brandy was

(Pl. 67) GEORGE II SAUCEPAN, Ann Craig and John Neville, London, 1742. The gourd shape of this piece and the beautifully engraved arms of William, second Baron Talbot, and his wife Mary de Cardonnel are fashionable precursors of the rococo style. Saucepans were employed to heat brandy at the table. In the 18th century flaming brandy was a favorite sauce. The substantial weight of this object was necessitated by the rigors of its intended use. (Height: 4 in.)

(Pl. 68) GEORGE II SAUCE BOAT, Dorothy Mills and Thomas Sarbitt, London, 1748. The hollow, flying-scroll handle is typical of the most elegant sauce boats of the mid-18th century, as are the early rococo, flat-chased C-scrolls. (Length: 5¼ in.)

(*Pl. 69*)  PAIR OF GEORGE II SAUCE BOATS, Elizabeth Godfrey, London, 1750. Extremely elegant, these heavy, shell-shaped sauce boats epitomize the combination of mass and fluidity of line characteristic of the best rococo designs. The importance of these pieces is further underscored by the fact that a virtually identical sauce boat appears on one of Godfrey's trade cards. (Length: 8¾ in.)

(*Fig. 24*)  Trade card of Elizabeth Godfrey which incorporates a silver sauce boat very similar to the pair in the museum's collection. Reproduced from *The London Goldsmiths, 1200–1800* by Ambrose Heal. (Courtesy of The British Museum)

E. Godfrey
Goldsmith, Silversmith,
AND
Jeweller;
at the Hand, Ring and Crown,
in Norris Street
St James's Hay-Market
Makes & Sells all sorts of Plate, Jewels, and
Watches, in the newest Taste at the most
Reasonable Rates.
N.B. All sorts of Second Hand Plate, Watches
&c. Bought and Sold

warmed to make it more flammable in a chafing dish over a spirit lamp or coals. The hot brandy and flames helped to reheat a serving dish that had cooled during its long trip from the kitchen. The 1742 date on this saucepan places it in the middle of Craig and Neville's brief partnership which lasted from 1740 to 1745.

Sauce boats, in pairs or larger sets, were found on every 18th-century dining table. Like salt dishes, most sauce boats were supported on three scroll feet which were cast and applied. These suited the oval shape of the standard sauce boat which had a long everted lip at one narrow end and a handle at the other. The most elegant mid-18th-century sauce boats, such as the one in this collection marked by Dorothy Mills and Thomas Sarbitt (pl. 68), had hollow, flying-scroll handles. The early rococo flat chasing of C-scrolls and flowers is consistent with the 1748 assay date.

Much more impressive are the pair of heavy, shell-shaped sauce boats marked two years later, in 1750, by Elizabeth Godfrey (pl. 69). These are much closer to French rococo in style than the more common three-footed type. Shell sauce boats similar to these were made by several major London silversmiths for their most fashionable and wealthy clients. They indicate the sophistication not only of the customer but of the silversmith herself. It is noteworthy that Elizabeth Godfrey depicted a very similar sauce boat on her trade card (fig. 24) in addition to several other equally ornate and stylish pieces of silver. Not surprisingly, Elizabeth Godfrey counted His Royal Highness the Duke of Cumberland among her patrons. Her maiden name—Pantin—indicates that she was raised in the tradition of Huguenot silversmithing, in the Westminster area, and, while perhaps not a practicing artisan, registered her own mark as a goldsmith after the death of both of her husbands.

Sauce tureens were introduced in Britain and Ireland during the 1760s and are a feature of the neoclassical and subsequent styles. The set of four rectangular sauce tureens marked in 1809 by Rebecca Emes and Edward Barnard (pl. 74) resemble covered entrée dishes of the period. The deep, oblong, tub shape was derived from Roman sarcophagi. The attractive handles were inspired by antique metalwork and the ball feet resemble those found on teapots around 1805. The regular gadrooned borders on the covers of these sauce tureens were made in a mechanical roller out of pre-drawn wire. These handsome pieces were, in fact, quite easily assembled from stock parts and offered little variety to either the client or the silversmith.

Some observers have suggested that sauce boats would not have been used for gravy as the silver handles, lacking any insulation, would have become too hot to touch. That argument is undermined by the fact that the sauce boats would have been accompanied by stands and ladles. Furthermore, the kitchen was often located hundreds of yards from the dining room and the gravy arrived at the table cool, or even cold. Certainly, hot liquid would cool quickly in these shallow, open vessels. These sauce boats were produced in considerable numbers, however, a fact which seems to indicate that they were used for whichever sauce or gravy was being consumed at the time.

During the latter half of the 18th century, the argyll was devised in an attempt to keep gravy really hot. These useful pieces either held hot water in an outer compartment or had a central cylindrical tube into which a heated iron rod was inserted. The argyll resembled a teapot, complete with cover, spout, and insulated handle. The Emes and Barnard example in the collection, which carries an 1811 assay letter, was a style available after about 1770 (pl. 71). The capacity of an argyll was quite small and rather few pieces seem to have been made, so the concern for hot gravy appears not to have been of overwhelming importance. During the fifty

(*Pl. 70*)  George III sauce boat, attributed to Elizabeth Muns, London, 1768. Muns appears to have worked for only one year after her husband died. (Length: 7⅜ in.)

Opposite: (*Pl. 71*)  Regency Argyll, Rebecca Emes and Edward Barnard, London, 1811. A heated iron rod inserted into the central cylinder of this piece kept gravy hot, and the low position of the spout allowed only the meat juice to be poured as the fat rose to the top. The raffia wrapped around the handle provided insulation. (Height: 4¾ in.)

years between 1770 and 1820 when argylls were prevalent, far more sets of sauce boats and sauce tureens were produced. Argylls are highly collectible today, largely because of their rarity.

Another unusual object in this collection associated with keeping food hot is the dish cross hallmarked in 1771 and attributed to Sarah Buttall (pl. 72). Dish crosses are among the few antique silver forms produced for the table which were always made as a single item rather than in pairs or in larger sets. Placed on sideboards or in the center of a dinner table, they supported a dish or bowl over a spirit lamp. They developed from earlier braziers (often called chafing dishes in America), which held hot coals. The arms of the dish cross terminate in movable brackets which were used to secure dishes of various sizes or shapes. The pierced, rococo, shell-shaped feet of the example illustrated continued to be used on dish crosses well into the neoclassical period. The dish brackets have been cleverly formed from loops of silver wire (fig. 25).

Another form which often was made as a single item rather than in multiples of two is the swing-handled basket. Although these large baskets are inherently fragile due to the way in which they have been pierced and their relatively light weight, they seem to have survived in large quantities, perhaps because they are so pretty and, in fact, not terribly useful. Their original purpose remains somewhat unclear.

Throughout the 1700s baskets of natural materials, such as straw and willow, were just as fashionable and common as they are today. The age of rococo appears to have taken particular delight in combining the look of woven wicker with the richest and most elaborate silver,

Right: (*Pl. 72*) GEORGE III DISH CROSS, attributed to Sarah Buttall, London, 1771. One of several devices created to keep food warm. The bars are adjustable, as are the pierced shell-shaped feet and looped-wire supports, to accommodate vessels of various dimensions. (Length of bar, tip to tip: 10¾ in.)

Below: (*Fig. 25*) Detail of movable bracket and foot of GEORGE III DISH CROSS attributed to Sarah Buttall.

porcelain, or glass. Silver baskets, shaped and pierced to imitate their humble wicker or straw counterparts, were sometimes referred to as cake, bread, or fruit baskets; they were probably used for all three purposes. The oval, flat-bottomed, open-work baskets of the early to mid-18th century were derived from 16th-century pieces and were certainly used for bread. Swing-handled silver baskets are known to have been given to churches around 1800, either for serving Communion bread or collecting contributions. In the late 18th century silver baskets also joined epergnes, elaborate stands with branching arms, as objects for the dessert table. It seems unlikely, however, that silver baskets were used by ladies to hold their sewing equipment, as some have suggested.

The light-weight silver basket bearing a 1788 date letter and Hester Bateman's mark has the characteristic gracefulness of line and attractive delicacy associated with the best Bateman silver (pl. 73). The free, looping arcs of the rim are particularly notable (fig. 26). The exceptionally wide pierced band is based on neoclassical vine and husk motifs, and the simple piercing of the foot adds to the sense of lightness. A band of molded reeding strengthens the rim and echoes the design of the handle, offering an appealing contrast to the sprightly piercing. This piece, which combines elegant design with the simplest of manufacturing techniques, embodies the characteristics that made the Bateman firm so successful.

Left: (*Pl. 73*) and detail below (*Fig. 26*) GEORGE III CAKE BASKET, Hester Bateman, London, 1788. This piece exudes confidence in its design, relying on beautiful lines and excellent crafting. The border (see detail below) is engraved with foliate scrolling, urns, and Prince of Wales feathers within bright-cut bands. Reeding adorns the edge and handle. (Length: $16\frac{1}{4}$ in.)

Overleaf: (*Pl. 74*) FOUR GEORGE III SAUCE TUREENS WITH COVERS, Rebecca Emes and Edward Barnard, London, 1809. Sauce tureens became popular alternatives to gravy boats during the neoclassical period. The form of these pieces, with their deep, oblong shape, is derived from Roman sarcophagi. (Height of each with cover: $5\frac{7}{8}$ in.)

Right: (*Pl. 75*) GEORGE IV CAKE BASKET, Rebecca Emes and Edward Barnard, London, 1827. The abundant, dense decoration is characteristic of the rococo-revival style popular in the second quarter of the 19th century. (Diameter: 11¼ in.)

Below: (*Fig. 27*) Detail of ram's head and swagged chains on cast legs of GEORGE III CENTERPIECE by Mary Troby.

Opposite: (*Pl. 76*) GEORGE III CENTERPIECE, Mary Troby, London, 1808. The simple lines of the silver stand are intended to set off the ornate, hand-cut crystal bowl. (Height of stand and bowl: 10 in.)

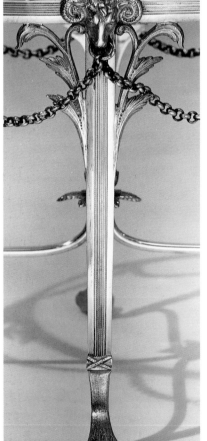

## 7. Dessert services

Dessert, consisting of beautiful, elaborate, and delicious confections based on fruit, might be served as the last of several courses at dinner or as an "entertainment" or party in its own right during the 18th century. From at least medieval, if not Roman, times it was just as important for dessert to please the eye as the palate. Special, highly decorative sets of china, glassware, and table ornaments were devised just for dessert, therefore. Since dessert services were the most expensively decorated of all tableware and were saved for special occasions, they have survived in greater numbers than the more mundane dinner services. In fact, much of the porcelain and glass seen today in antique shops and museums are from dessert, rather than dinner, services.

Silversmiths also designed special objects, ranging from miniature temples of love to epergnes and serving dishes in fanciful shapes, for the dessert table of the 18th and early 19th centuries. The custom of setting the dinner table in a symmetrical pattern with dozens of oval and circular dishes resulted in a table with a horizontal emphasis. By the late 18th century, however, the dessert course had taken on a vertical accent, and stands and vessels were invented to provide height. The silver dessert dish marked by Rebecca Emes and Edward Barnard in 1827 (pl. 75) probably came from such a set, since "corner pieces" were considered just as important as a "center piece." Often sets of two or four pedestaled dishes of different heights were produced. This footed dish is designed in the rococo-revival style, which tended to include the flower and scroll motifs of the mid-18th century in greater profusion. The scalloped, paneled form and encrusted floral effect of this piece reproduce the style of such 19th-century English porcelain makers as Rockingham and Coalport. Indeed, this silver stand undoubtedly would have been used with a large set of such dessert china. Since fruit in a variety of forms—fresh, stewed, dried, or candied—always appeared on the dessert table, this piece was intended, no doubt, to hold a pyramid of plums, strawberries, grapes, or other similar

Right: (*Pl. 77*) and detail below (*Pl. 78*)  *Marriage à la Mode: The Countess's Morning Levée* (1743–45) by William Hogarth (1697–1764). This humorous scene illustrates the wide variety of activities that could take place in a lady's closet or dressing-room during the morning hours. The Countess displays a few silver objects on her dressing table. Her child's silver coral-and-bells hangs from a sash draped over her chair. (Reproduced by courtesy of the Trustees, The National Gallery, London)

delicacies. The lavish decoration lends visual richness to the piece, while the shaped panels and repoussé work permit the use of a relatively thin gauge of silver.

The oval, silver frame marked by Mary Troby in 1808 (pl. 76) which holds a cut-glass bowl was probably one of a matching set for serving fruit, as was the Emes and Barnard footed dish discussed earlier. The cast legs with applied ram's-head masks, from which a simple silver chain is swagged (fig. 27), are a rather late interpretation of ancient Roman metal furniture. The linear, open design of the stand complements the clear-glass bowl beautifully.

## 8. Breakfast services

Tea, dinner, and dessert were not the only meals at which our ancestors entertained. Even breakfast was not always a private affair during the 18th century. It was quite fashionable for enlightened ladies to offer food and drink to everyone from the hairdresser to the priest in the small, intimate rooms known as closets or dressing-rooms. Here they spent the morning dressing, applying cosmetics, talking, embroidering, or writing letters. William Hogarth captures many of these activities with his usual satirical brilliance in *Marriage à la Mode: The Countess's Morning Levée* from 1743–45 (pls. 77 and 78). No wonder the well-off displayed silver or gold dressing-table accessories as symbols of their status, just as Hogarth's countess does. It later became customary in the large country houses for ladies to be served a light breakfast in bed, while gentlemen helped themselves to heartier fare laid out in a special room set aside for that purpose.

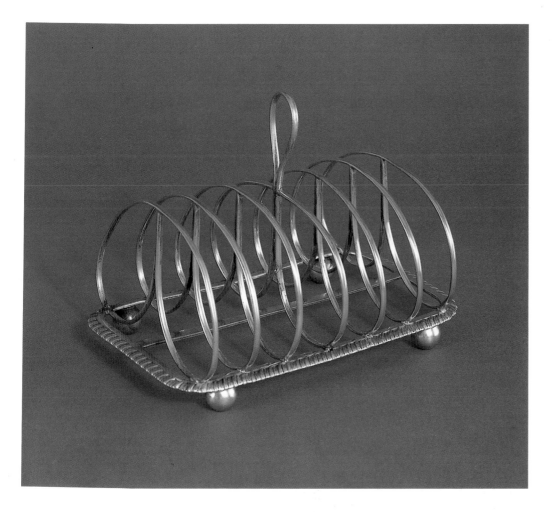

(*Pl. 79*)  REGENCY TOAST RACK, Rebecca Emes and Edward Barnard, London, 1817. Toast racks developed as part of the 19th-century service for buffet breakfasts. With its functional and innovative use of silver wire, this rack bears a strong resemblance to the bentwood furniture that became popular a few years later. (Length: $6\frac{1}{4}$ in.)

103

Right: (*Pl. 80*) and detail of handle below (*Fig. 28*) GEORGE III EGG CODDLER ON LAMP STAND, Rebecca Emes and William Emes; Rebecca Emes and Edward Barnard, London, 1808. The marks on the pot, rack, and stand of this piece reflect the sequence of Emes's partners. The mark on the pot is that of Rebecca Emes and William Emes, with whom she was a partner for just over three months. The mark on the egg rack, however, is that of Emes and Barnard, her long-term associate. The small hourglass attached to the stem of the rack, which protrudes through the coddler's lids, timed the cooking eggs. (Height of body and rack: 9¼ in.; Height of stand: 3⅜ in.)

Opposite: (*Pl. 81*) The intriguing GEORGE III EGG CODDLER ON LAMP STAND (1808) by Rebecca Emes, William Emes, and Edward Barnard has an hourglass to time the eggs. The Emes and Barnard REGENCY TOAST RACK (1817) could be used in a breakfast buffet, as could Ann Robertson's GEORGE III FISH SLICE (*ca.* 1801). The GEORGE III SALT CELLAR (1782) is by Anne Smith and Nathaniel Appleton and the VICTORIAN SALT SPOON (1849) by Elizabeth Eaton.

Always responsive to new trends, silversmiths designed pieces for informal, help-yourself breakfasts, such as the silver-wire toast rack marked in 1817 by Rebecca Emes and Edward Barnard (pl. 79) or the curious egg coddler, also by Emes and Barnard (pl. 80). Useful rather than decorative, the coddler consists of a spirit lamp, pot of water, and rack to hold egg cups (now missing). The miniature hourglass on the top of the rack determined how long the eggs were to be boiled in the sarcophagus-shaped pot. Cooking one's own eggs at the breakfast table or in the bedroom may have been a clever idea, but in practice it must have been rather messy and unsatisfactory. Few silver egg coddlers survive. In fact, the egg cups for the Emes and Barnard piece probably were removed long ago to be put to more practical use in the kitchen and pantry.

This egg coddler has a number of interesting marks which provide information about Rebecca Emes's career. Rebecca's husband, the successful silversmith John Emes, is presumed to have died shortly before June 30, 1808, when Rebecca Emes entered her mark at

Goldsmiths' Hall in partnership with William Emes, who may have been the executor of John's estate and Rebecca's brother-in-law. The mark of Rebecca and William Emes and the 1808 date letter appear on the bottom of the body or pot for this egg coddler. The pot may well have been a stock part which was marked before being finished as an egg coddler, sauce tureen, or even a teapot. In any case, that mark was used for only three-and-a-half months. On October 14, 1808, Rebecca Emes entered into partnership with Edward Barnard and her second mark appears on the bottom of the rack. The lamp, lamp stand, and pot covers bear only the 1808 date letter and the lion-passant sterling marks. It is likely that this unusual item was constructed between about September and November 1808 during the transition in the business following John Emes's death. The esoteric purpose of this piece is consistent with the high quality of Emes and Barnard silver that was produced for a fashion-conscious and rather aristocratic clientele. The lion's head handles, a decorative motif characteristic of the period, reinforce the simple elegance of this unusual object (fig. 28).

9. Small flatware

Although large hollow ware pieces make a more impressive display of silver in a museum and unquestionably present a maker's skill to the best advantage, many—perhaps most—early silversmiths made their living producing conventional flatware or other small forms of silver. Certainly, most women who were actually involved in the craft of silversmithing made spoons or contributed to some aspect of the smallworker's or jeweler's art in which dexterity compensated for the lack of physical strength. Indeed, many women worked as chainmakers, chasers, engravers, or finishers.

For example, the techniques needed to create the 1808 child's coral-and-bells, attributed to Mary Ann Croswell, are the skills of a jeweler rather than a large plateworker (pl. 82).

(Pl. 84)  *Portrait of Sir Thomas Cave Bt., and His Family in the Grounds of Stanford Hall, Leicestershire* (1749) by Arthur Devis (*ca.* 1711–87). This painting illustrates the more formal approach to entertaining a child with a silver coral-and-bells. (Courtesy of a private collector)

This all-purpose infant's toy contains a stick of coral for teething, a cluster of bells, and a silver shaft terminating in a whistle. The delicately engraved decoration dates this example to the neoclassical period, although this type of pacifier was made from the 17th through the 19th centuries. Coral-and-bells, or teething sticks as they were prosaically known, were so expensive to buy that it has been suggested they were worn by the mother or nurse and used only occasionally by the infant or young child. Some paintings of the period, such as *Portrait of Sir Thomas Cave Bt., and His Family in the Grounds of Stanford Hall, Leicestershire* by Arthur Devis (pls. 84 and 85), in which the mother holds the coral-and-bells, would seem to confirm this supposition. Other paintings depict coral-and-bells suspended from ribbons or chains around the necks or waists of young children, however, as in Hogarth's portrait *Lord Grey and Lady Mary West as Children* (pl. 83). Coral has long been thought to promote health and increase good fortune. In the days of high infant mortality, it is understandable that mothers tried every means at their disposal to protect their children. Even the Puritans, known to disapprove of jewelry, hung strings of coral beads on their young children. It is certainly appropriate for a woman silversmith to be associated with this intimate, childhood toy. Coral-and-bells appear to have been the only standard silver or gold item produced solely for the benefit of children.

## 10. Small boxes

Small silver boxes designed for a variety of purposes were often made by silversmiths who specialized in such forms. Flat, oval containers used for carrying tobacco, which was either

Opposite: (*Pl. 85*) Detail of *Portrait of Sir Thomas Cave Bt., and His Family in the Grounds of Stanford Hall, Leicestershire* by Arthur Devis.

(*Pl. 86*) WILLIAM III OVAL TOBACCO BOX, Elizabeth Haselwood, Norwich, *ca.* 1695. This, the oldest piece in the collection, formerly was on exhibition at the Norwich Castle Museum. The coat of arms on the cover belongs to the Gedding family, Norfolk. Later than the box itself, it is probably that of the third or fourth generation of owners. (Length: $3\frac{3}{4}$ in.)

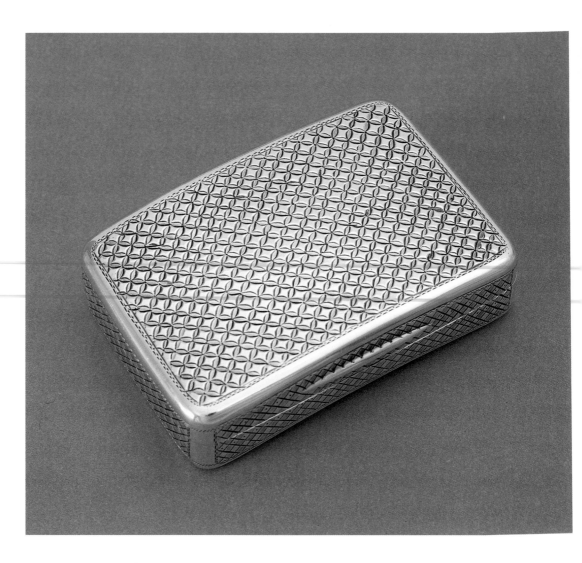

*(Pl. 87)* GEORGE III SNUFF BOX, Alice Burrows and George Burrows II, London, 1802. Fairly flat snuff boxes with curved sides for easy insertion into the pockets of gentlemen's tightly fitting trousers were a popular variation in the shape of snuff boxes in the early 19th century. (Length: $3\frac{1}{8}$ in.)

grated for snuff or smoked in a pipe, were the most common type of 18th-century silver box. The oldest piece of silver in the collection dates from *ca.* 1695 and is an oval tobacco box marked by Elizabeth Haselwood (pl. 86). The T.B. pricked inside the cover is probably an original engraving. The rococo coat of arms of the Gedding family of Norfolk on the exterior, however, probably belongs to the third or fourth owners. Both women and men of the middle and upper classes used this type of tobacco box. These relatively inexpensive boxes were frequently presented as gifts and prizes.

Alice and George Burrows II marked a silver snuff box in 1802 (pl. 87), more than a hundred years after the Haselwood example. The rectangular form, the long sides of which have been slightly curved to fit the pocket of a gentleman's fashionably tight trousers, was a new variation in shape. The overall engraved diaper pattern was a sensible way of disguising the scratches acquired through frequent use. By the 19th century fewer ladies were indulging in snuff or pipes, but box makers continued to make similar, but much smaller, silver containers for smelling salts, scented vinegar (the air freshener of the day), pills, trinkets, and cosmetics. Box makers of this period also made nutmeg graters resembling small boxes.

The box made by Jane Williams and Carden Terry of Cork, Ireland, in 1814 (pl. 88) is a fine example of a rare Irish Freedom Box. Centuries ago, when walled cities functioned as

(*Pl. 88*) and detail of engraved cover below (*Fig. 29*) REGENCY IRISH FREEDOM BOX, Jane Williams and Carden Terry, Cork, 1814. Freedom boxes replaced the "key to the city" in Ireland, honoring recipients and conferring the "freedom" of a city. The engravings on the lid (see detail below) include Irish harps and the arms of the city of Cork. The box was formerly in the collection of Henry P. McIllhenny of Philadelphia. (Length: $3\frac{7}{8}$ in.)

(*Pl. 89*) GEORGE III TABLESPOON (top), Ann Bateman and Peter Bateman, London, 1795. Fashioned in the Old English style. (Length: 8¾ in.) GEORGE III TABLESPOON (middle), attributed to Elizabeth Tookey, London, 1771. The ridged, rounded edges of the handle are characteristic of the Hanoverian style. (Length: 7⅞ in.) GEORGE IV DESSERT SPOON (bottom), Sarah Blake and John William Blake, London, 1820. An example of the fiddle pattern. (Length: 7¼ in.)

Opposite: (*Pl. 90*) SET OF FOUR GEORGE II DESSERT SPOONS (top), attributed to Elizabeth Tookey, London, 1740. (Length: 8¼ in.) PAIR OF GEORGE II TABLESPOONS (bottom), attributed to Elizabeth Tookey, London, 1740. (Length: 8¾ in.)

individual states, it was a great honor to be presented with a key to a city gate, which signified the freedom to enter or leave the city without permission. While the custom still prevails, it has sadly degenerated into a silly and nonsensical exercise involving movie stars or athletes and huge plywood or Styrofoam keys. In the late 17th century the Irish wisely began presenting silver boxes of a size and shape suitable for eventual use as tobacco boxes, accompanied by a parchment officially conferring the "freedom" of the city on the chosen individual. These delightful little boxes, usually decorated with the arms of the city, certainly were more useful than a key. In addition to the arms of Cork, the border of this box includes Irish harps in its charming design (fig. 29). Jane Williams is the only known woman silversmith from Cork. She worked with her talented father, Carden Terry, after she was widowed. Her husband, John Williams, had served his apprenticeship with Terry. Many pieces marked by Jane Williams and Carden Terry, like this box, are well engraved.

11. Spoons

Although not particularly interesting visually, spoons were undoubtedly the most common pieces of silver made by women silversmiths. The fine examples in this collection are representative of the very limited styles available to most 18th- and 19th-century customers.

(*Pl. 91*)  SIX WILLIAM IV
TABLESPOONS, Mary Chawner,
London, 1835. Fiddle pattern.
(Length: 8¾ in.) TWO VICTORIAN
DINNER FORKS, Mary Chawner,
London, 1839. These are examples of
a style known as "French tipped."
Chawner specialized in spoons and
forks. (Length: 8¼ in.)

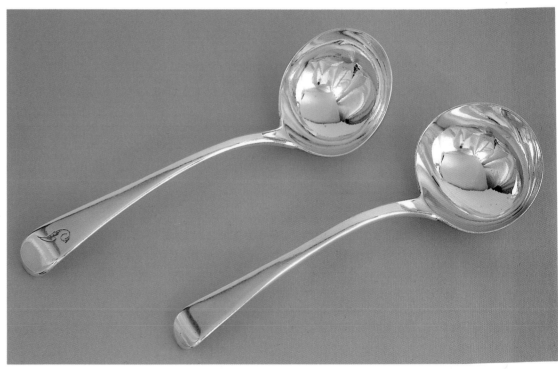

(*Pl. 92*) SIX REGENCY TEASPOONS, Sarah Blake and John William Blake, London, 1812. Old English pattern. The terminals are engraved with initials. (Length: $5\frac{1}{2}$ in.)

(*Pl. 93*) GEORGE III SAUCE LADLE (top), Ann Bateman and Peter Bateman, London, 1797. Old English pattern. (Length: 7 in.) GEORGE IV SAUCE LADLE (bottom), Sarah Blake and John William Blake, London, 1821. Old English pattern. (Length: $6\frac{7}{8}$ in.)

(*Pl. 94*)  GEORGE III TEA CADDY
SPOON (top left), Elizabeth Morley,
London, 1798. (Length: $3\frac{3}{8}$ in.)
GEORGE III TEA CADDY SPOON
(top middle), Elizabeth Morley,
London, 1797. (Length: $2\frac{1}{2}$ in.)
Because so many caddy spoons had
pretty, shell-shaped bowls, the form
itself was often called a "caddy
shell." GEORGE III TEA CADDY
SPOON (top right), Ann Bateman
and Peter Bateman, London, 1797.
(Length: 3 in.) VICTORIAN SALT
SPOON (bottom), Elizabeth Eaton,
London, 1849. (Length: $4\frac{1}{4}$ in.)

Silver forks were not bought in any number by the middle class until well into the 19th century, and silver spoons represented the most luxurious item of tableware which many people possessed. Tablespoons were needed by the dozen for the 18th-century dinner table (pl. 91). Large spoons (pls. 89 and 90) were practical for eating everything from soup and stew to pudding and porridge. Tea (pl. 92) and coffee spoons, designed to fit popular cup sizes, were symbols of gentility. Throughout the 18th century few specialized flatware forms were produced for serving food and most of those that did emerge, such as ladles, caddy shells, and marrow scoops (pls. 93, 94, and 96), were merely variations on the spoon.

## 12. Specialized eating utensils

The general increase in disposable income and emphasis on good manners during the 19th century resulted in more and more specialized eating utensils. This trend reached ridiculous proportions in the United States at the end of the century when more than one hundred different silver flatware implements were available in thousands of different patterns. The Victorian English were more restrained and sensible in their concern for politeness at the table, but the move toward special forms may be seen, nonetheless, in the three fish slices by Mary Chawner and Ann Robertson (pl. 97) and the asparagus tongs by Elizabeth Eaton in this collection.

(Pl. 95) VICTORIAN ASPARAGUS TONGS, Elizabeth Eaton, London, 1852. These tongs are an example of the threaded-shell pattern. Asparagus tongs originated in the 18th century, as part of the trend toward specialized utensils for serving delicacies. Tongs such as these may well have been used for serving pastries and other foods in addition to asparagus. (Length: 9⅞ in.)

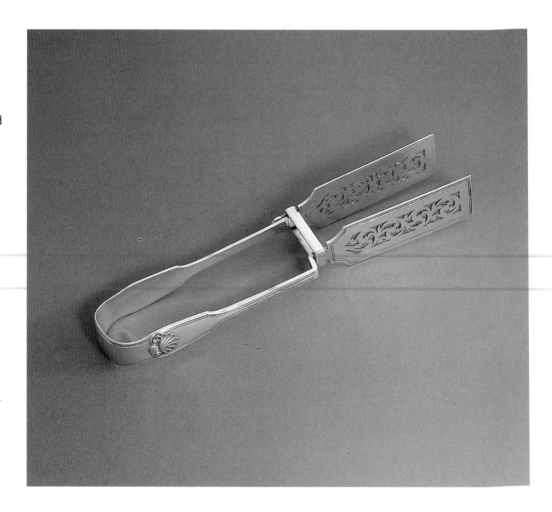

Fish slices, with a wide, pierced blade and a silver or bone handle, evolved in the mid-18th century as one of the first specialized table implements. The French rococo fish server, with a small, oval blade and long handle, probably was brought to England by Huguenot silver-smiths. Early British and Irish fish slices have rather large, triangular blades. Later examples may have blades shaped like a trowel, rectangle, leaf, fish, or designed in a wide variety of asymmetrical shapes. Some of these pieces appear to have been used for serving such foods as puddings and tarts in addition to fish.

Asparagus tongs also emerged during the 18th century in an early effort to develop specialized utensils for foods that were considered delicacies. The pair of tongs marked by Eaton in 1852 (pl. 95) are very typical of 19th-century tongs with their wide, pierced blades and fiddle-shell pattern on the arms. Such tongs may well have been used as an all-purpose serving implement for sandwiches, pastries, and pieces of meat in addition to asparagus spears.

*Conclusion*

It is important to remember that the objects in this collection—fine pieces by Hester Bateman, Rebecca Emes, Elizabeth Godfrey, Louisa Courtauld, and others—were put together in a remarkably short period of time, from a limited number of sources, according to the tastes and resources of one individual. As a collection, it does not attempt to represent the work of women silversmiths in general or of any one silversmith in particular. Nor does it attempt to include examples of every style or form. However, it is possible to draw some tentative conclusions.

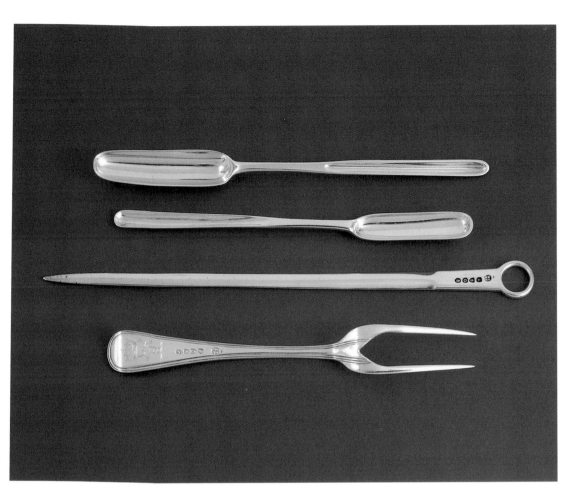

(Pl. 96) REGENCY MARROW SCOOP (top), Mary and Eliza Sumner, London, 1812. (Length: 9⅛ in.) GEORGE III MARROW SCOOP (middle), Jane Williams and Carden Terry, Cork, *ca.* 1810. This piece is marked "Sterling," a word which in the 18th century appeared only on Irish silver from the counties of Cork or Limerick. (Length: 8¼ in.) REGENCY MEAT SKEWER, Mary and Eliza Sumner, London, 1811. Used in the serving, not cooking, of meat or fowl. (Length: 11⅛ in.) REGENCY MEAT FORK, Mary and Eliza Sumner, London, 1814. (Length: 8¼ in.)

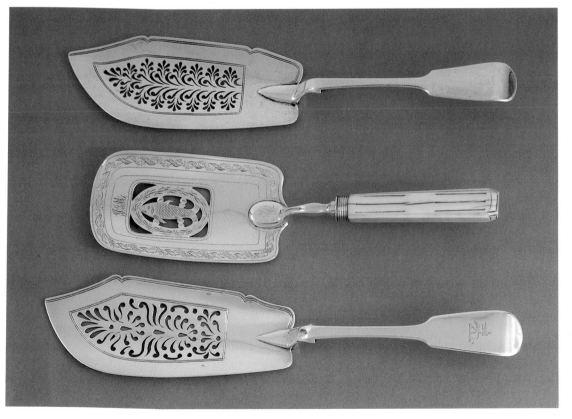

(Pl. 97) WILLIAM IV FISH SLICE (top), Mary Chawner, London, 1835. Fiddle pattern. (Length: 12¼ in.) GEORGE III FISH SLICE (middle), Ann Robertson, Newcastle upon Tyne, *ca.* 1801. Early form, with ivory handle. (Length: 10¾ in.) VICTORIAN FISH SLICE (bottom), Mary Chawner, London, 1839. Fiddle pattern. (Length: 12⅞ in.) Fish slices were among the earliest specialized serving utensils, and were sometimes used to serve pudding and other foods in addition to fish.

Below: (*Pl. 98*) and detail opposite (*Pl. 99*) *The Gough Family* (1741) by William Verelst (active 1734–*ca.* 1756). In addition to displaying the Gough family's obvious wealth, built upon trade with China and India, the painting also underscores the social and economic importance accorded to the preparation and consumption of tea. (Courtesy of a private collector; Photo John Webb)

Certainly the women represented in the collection worked within the stylistic and qualitative demands of their period and craft. Whether practicing silversmiths themselves or the managers of shops, these women were all thoroughly familiar with the techniques of the silver trade, and reached the high standard of artistry required by the Goldsmiths' Guild and the public. Those with the skills and opportunities to attract wealthier customers provided more fashionable, well-made wares. Those whose businesses relied on volume exploited industrial developments and stylistic short cuts effectively. Overall, however, the collection demonstrates that British women have earned a place in the history of silversmithing. Not only have they run successful businesses, they have also produced work that has been, and will continue to be, highly valued and admired.

(*Fig. 30*) The top portion of the first page for the letter *S* in the first Largeworkers' Register showing the entry for Alice Sheene on April 29, 1700. (Courtesy of the Worshipful Company of Goldsmiths)

# Biographical List of British and Irish Women Silversmiths

Compiled by Catherine Drillis, Philippa Glanville, and Nancy Valentine

*Note:* In Britain and Ireland during the 17th, 18th, and 19th centuries women's identities were determined largely by the men in their lives—fathers, husbands, sons. Several prominent silversmiths like Anne Tanqueray probably received training in their fathers' workshop, and later married their fathers' apprentices. In most cases, women silversmiths did not register their mark until after their husbands' deaths. Even then, they often registered a mark in partnership with a son, son-in-law, brother, or journeyman. The category "Marital status at registration" provides the information currently available on this aspect of women silversmiths' careers.

Asterisks (*) following the name denote silversmiths represented in the museum's collection.

*Name:* ABRAHAMS, JUDITH
*Location:* Deal
*Classification:* Silversmith
*Other classifications:* Jeweler, dealer in old clothes
*Date mark registered:* Unknown
*Active:* ca. 1814
*Marital status at registration:* Unknown
*Address:* Beach Street
*Source:* Sun Insurance 11937, vol. 110
*Additional information:* Sun Insurance Policy No. 900067, registered October 28, 1814: on stock, utensils, and plate £900, jewelry £100.

*Name:* ADAMS, ANN
*Maiden name:* Cottin
*Location:* Exeter
*Classification:* Goldsmith
*Date mark registered:* Unknown
*Active:* Pre-1830
*Marital status at registration:* Widow
*In partnership with:* Edward Hewish Adams (son)
*Husband's name:* John Adams
*Husband's classification:* Goldsmith
*Source:* Kent notes for Jackson
*Additional information:* Daughter of Thomas Cottin II, goldsmith. John Adams died in 1806. Ann Adams died in 1830.

*Name:* ADAMS, ELIZABETH
*Location:* London
*Classification:* Platemaker
*Date mark registered:* June 13, 1823
*Marital status at registration:* Unknown
*In partnership with:* Charles Hastings Rich
*Address:* St Ann's Lane
*Source:* Grimwade, p. 419

*Name:* ALDRIDGE, ELIZABETH
*Maiden name:* Parker
*Location:* London
*Classification:* Unknown
*Date mark registered:* 1766–67
*Marital status at registration:* Widow
*Address:* St. Leonard, Foster Lane
*Husband's name:* Edward Aldridge I
*Husband's classification:* Largeworker, clothworker
*Source:* Grimwade, p. 421

*Name:* ALUMBRIDGE, ANN
*Location:* Sherborne
*Classification:* Goldsmith
*Date mark registered:* Unknown
*Marital status at registration:* Unknown
*Source:* Sun Insurance 11936, vol. 10, p. 238
*Additional information:* Sun Insurance Policy No. 16238, registered January 12, 1719.

*Name:* AMBROSE, JANE
*Location:* London
*Classification:* Watchmaker
*Date mark registered:* Unknown
*Marital status at registration:* Unknown
*Address:* 202 Oxford Street
*Husband's name:* John Ambrose
*Husband's classification:* Watchmaker
*Source:* Sun Insurance Policy, vol. 440
*Additional information:* Sun Insurance Policy No. 809369, registered October 29, 1807: on house, wearing apparel, plate, and books £380, utensils and stock £250, china and glass £20.

*Name:* ANDREWS, ANN
*Location:* London
*Classification:* Smallworker
*Date mark registered:* March 26, 1759
*Marital status at registration:* Wife or widow
*Address:* Brick Lane, Old Street
*Husband's name:* John Andrews I

Husband's classification: Smallworker
Source: Grimwade, p. 423
Additional information: Second mark registered
June 27, 1760; third June 16, 1761.

Name: ANDREWS, ELIZABETH
Location: London
Classification: Goldsmith
Date mark registered: Unknown
Marital status at registration: Widow
In partnership with: Charles Aldridge
Address: 85 Cornhill
Husband's name: George Andrews
Source: Grimwade, p. 421; Sun Insurance
11936, vol. 398, p. 62
Additional information: Sun Insurance Policy No.
619288, registered August 29, 1793: on
household goods in dwelling house £80,
wearing apparel £40, utensils and stock
£2,900. Partnership with Charles Aldridge
dissolved in 1793.

Name: APPLEBEE, JANE
Location: Falmouth
Classification: Goldsmith
Date mark registered: Unknown
Marital status at registration: Widow
Source: Sun Insurance 11936, vol. 6, p. 274
Additional information: Sun Insurance Policy No.
8526, registered June 17, 1717: on the dwelling
house of Thomas Poole.

Name: ASHE, MARY
Alternative spellings: Ash
Location: Launceston
Classification: Unknown
Date mark registered: November 13, 1703
Active: ca. 1693–1722
Marital status at registration: Widow
Husband's name: Richard Ashe
Husband's classification: Goldsmith
Source: Kent notes for Jackson
Additional information: Mary Ashe registered her
mark in Exeter. Richard Ashe died in 1689.
She died in 1722.

Name: ASHWORTH, MARY
Maiden name: Landell
Alternative spellings: Mercy
Location: Durham
Classification: Ironmonger
Date mark registered: 1785
Active: 1785–1803
Marital status at registration: Widow
Address: Market Place
Husband's name: Michael Ashworth
Husband's classification: Ironmonger and banker

Source: Gill, p. 48
Additional information: Sent silver to be engraved
by Beilby & Bewick between 1782 and 1790.
Second mark registered July 28, 1792. Michael
Ashworth died in 1776. Mary Ashworth died
in 1822 at the age of eighty-eight.

Name: ATKINS, MARY
Location: London
Classification: Casemaker
Date mark registered: November 16, 1811 (incuse
mark)
Marital status at registration: Unknown
Address: 14 Bridgewater Square
Source: Grimwade, p. 313

Name: ATKINS, THEODOSIA ANN
Location: London
Classification: Smallworker
Date mark registered: September 27, 1815
Marital status at registration: Widow
Address: Well Street, Cripplegate
Husband's name: James Atkins
Husband's classification: Bucklemaker
Source: Grimwade, p. 427

Name: AVELINE, LAURA
Location: London
Classification: Casemaker (?)
Date mark registered: October 12, 1772 (incuse
mark)
Marital status at registration: Unknown
Address: Denmark Street, St. Giles
Source: Grimwade, p. 312

Name: AVELINE, MARY
Location: London
Classification: Casemaker
Date mark registered: July 19, 1779 (incuse
mark)
Marital status at registration: Unknown
In partnership with: Gideon Macaire
Address: 5 Denmark Street, St. Giles
Source: Grimwade, p. 313

Name: AVERY, EDITH
Maiden name: Orchard
Second married name: Jouet
Location: Exeter
Classification: Goldsmith
Date mark registered: Used her first husband's
mark
Marital status at registration: Widow
Husband's name: John Avery
Husband's classification: Goldsmith
Source: Kent notes for Jackson

*Additional information:* John Avery died in 1703. Her second husband was Peter Jouet (m. 1706), who was also a goldsmith and may have been her journeyman. Other addresses: Topsham, Devon, post-1706; London, 1723.

*Name:* BAINBRIDGE, ELIZABETH
*Location:* Dublin
*Classification:* Watchmaker
*Date mark registered:* Unknown
*Active:* ca. 1802
*Marital status at registration:* Unknown
*Address:* 54 Bolton Street
*Source:* Bennett (1972), p. 294

*Name:* BAINBRIDGE, HARRIET
*Location:* London
*Classification:* Smallworker
*Date mark registered:* August 22, 1831
*Marital status at registration:* Widow
*Address:* 35 Holborn Hill
*Husband's name:* William Bainbridge II
*Husband's classification:* Smallworker
*Source:* Grimwade, p. 428

*Name:* BAINBRIDGE, MARY
*Location:* London
*Classification:* Largeworker
*Date mark registered:* April 21, 1707
*Marital status at registration:* Widow (?)
*Address:* Oat Lane
*Husband's name:* William Bainbridge I (?)
*Husband's classification:* Goldsmith (?)
*Source:* Grimwade, p. 428

*Name:* BAKER, MRS.
*Location:* Dublin
*Classification:* Unknown
*Date mark registered:* Unknown
*Active:* ca. 1725
*Marital status at registration:* Unknown
*Source:* Bennett (1972), p. 294
*Additional information:* Sent a lot of plate to be assayed. Possibly mother or wife of Richard Baker, freeman 1711–30. The mark *RB* shown under her entry.

*Name:* BARKER, MARY
*Location:* Birmingham
*Classification:* Repairer
*Other classifications:* Buttonmaker, smallworker
*Date mark registered:* Unknown
*Active:* 1801 onward
*Marital status at registration:* Unknown
*In partnership with:* Creed
*Address:* Crego Street, Holloway Head

*Source:* Jones, p. 306
*Additional information:* By 1860 the firm was known as Barker Bros. under the directorship of William and Matthias Barker.

*Name:* BARKER, SUSANNA*
*Alternative spellings:* Susannah
*Location:* London
*Classification:* Smallworker
*Date mark registered:* June 25, 1778
*Active:* 1778–ca. 1793
*Marital status at registration:* Unknown
*Address:* 16 Gutter Lane
*Source:* Grimwade, p. 430; Heal, p. 101
*Additional information:* Heal records her as a working goldsmith at 29 Gutter Lane from 1790 to 1793. Second mark registered August 12, 1789; third August 26, 1789. Barker specialized in making wine labels.

*Name:* BARNETT, ELIZABETH
*Location:* London
*Classification:* Hiltmaker
*Date mark registered:* February 11, 1823
*Marital status at registration:* Widow
*Address:* 36 Cock Lane, Smithfield
*Husband's name:* Michael Barnett
*Husband's classification:* Smallworker, hiltmaker
*Source:* Grimwade, p. 431

*Name:* BARRETT, MARY
*Location:* Dublin
*Classification:* Silversmith
*Date mark registered:* Unknown
*Active:* 1722–30
*Marital status at registration:* Widow
*Husband's name:* Edward Barrett
*Husband's classification:* Silversmith
*Source:* Bennett (1984), p. 139
*Additional information:* She continued to use her husband's *EB* punch. Edward Barrett died in 1722.

*Name:* BARROWS, ELIZABETH
*Location:* London
*Classification:* Bucklemaker
*Date mark registered:* March 6, 1789
*Marital status at registration:* Unknown
*In partnership with:* Jane Williams
*Address:* 8 Bedford Street, The Strand
*Source:* Grimwade, p. 389

*Name:* BARUGH, ANN
*Alternative spellings:* Burugh
*Location:* London
*Classification:* Smallworker, casemaker

*Date mark registered:* August 30, 1721 (incuse mark)
*Marital status at registration:* Widow
*Address:* Bolt Court, Fleet Street
*Husband's name:* John Barugh
*Husband's classification:* Clockmaker, smallworker
*Source:* Grimwade, p. 432
*Additional information:* Second mark registered December 12, 1731.

*Name:* BASS, MARY
*Location:* London
*Classification:* Unknown
*Date mark registered:* Unknown
*Active:* Apprenticeship—1708–17
*Marital status at registration:* Spinster (?)
*Source:* Smith, p. 68
*Additional information:* Goldsmiths' Hall Apprentice Register, vol. 5, p. 3 (1708). Freed by service July 18, 1717. Later married Michael Hatton.

*Name:* BATEMAN, ANN*
*Maiden name:* Dowling
*Location:* London
*Classification:* Silversmith
*Other classifications:* Silverflatter
*Date mark registered:* May 2, 1791
*Active:* 1791–1805
*Marital status at registration:* Widow
*In partnership with:* 1) Peter Bateman (brother-in-law); 2) Peter and William Bateman (son)
*Address:* 108 Bunhill Row
*Husband's name:* Jonathan Bateman
*Husband's classification:* Silversmith
*Source:* Grimwade, p. 433; Sun Insurance policies
*Additional information:* Jonathan Bateman died on April 19, 1791. Ann Bateman was born in 1748 and died before 1813. Second mark, in partnership with Peter and William Bateman, registered January 1800. Sun Insurance Policy No. 626754, registered April 11, 1794: £1,000 total. Sun Insurance Policy No. 735426, registered August 7, 1802: £3,000 on company, £4,200 total. Sun Insurance Policy No. 839201, registered January 1, 1810: on house and counting house £1,000, engine house £1,300, workshop £200, house at 107 Bunhill Row in tenure of William Bateman £500.

*Name:* BATEMAN, HESTER*
*Maiden name:* Neden
*Alternative spellings:* Needham
*Location:* London
*Classification:* Smallworker

*Other classifications:* Goldsmith, spoonmaker, plateworker
*Date mark registered:* April 16, 1761
*Active:* 1761–90
*Marital status at registration:* Widow
*Address:* 107 Bunhill Row
*Husband's name:* John Bateman
*Husband's classification:* Chainmaker
*Source:* Grimwade, pp. 433, 733
*Additional information:* Second mark registered January 9, 1771; third June 17, 1774 (spoonmaker); fourth December 3, 1774 (plateworker); fifth June 5, 1776 (spoonmaker); sixth February 21, 1778 (spoonmaker); seventh November 25, 1781 (spoonmaker); eighth June 28, 1787 (plateworker); final August 3, 1787 (plateworker). She was listed as a goldsmith in the Parliamentary Report of 1773. Hester Bateman was born in 1708 and died on September 16, 1794. She married John Bateman on May 20, 1732. He died in 1760. Her apprentice, Crispin Fuller, married her granddaughter Sarah Clarke.

*Name:* BAXTER, SARAH
*Location:* London
*Classification:* Bucklemaker
*Date mark registered:* May 20, 1790
*Marital status at registration:* Widow (?)
*Address:* 47 Monkwell Street
*Source:* Grimwade, p. 399

*Name:* BEEDALL, MARY
*Location:* London
*Classification:* Bucklemaker
*Date mark registered:* March 22, 1780
*Marital status at registration:* Widow (?)
*In partnership with:* William Yardley
*Address:* 23 Thorney Street, Bloomsbury
*Husband's name:* Samuel Beedall (?)
*Source:* Grimwade, p. 398

*Name:* BELL, LYDIA
*Location:* London
*Classification:* Silversmith
*Date mark registered:* Unknown
*Active:* ca. 1765
*Marital status at registration:* Widow (?)
*Source:* Prideaux, vol. 2, p. 249
*Additional information:* Goldsmiths' Company Court of Assistants records, December 19, 1765.

*Name:* BELL, MARGARET
*Location:* Newcastle upon Tyne
*Classification:* Silversmith

*Other classifications:* Jeweler
*Date mark registered:* Unknown
*Active:* 1741–1838
*Marital status at registration:* Widow
*Address:* 10 Dean Street
*Husband's name:* James Bell (?)
*Source:* Gill, p. 62
*Additional information:* James Bell died in 1838.

*Name:* BELL, MARY
*Maiden name:* Young (?)
*Location:* London
*Classification:* Watchmaker
*Date mark registered:* Unknown
*Marital status at registration:* Unknown
*Address:* 5 Baynes Row in Cold Bath Fields
*Source:* Sun Insurance 11936, vol. 374, p. 119
*Additional information:* Sun Insurance Policy No.
578071, registered January 1, 1791: on dwelling
house £150, wearing apparel £100, utensils
and stock £50.

*Name:* BENCE, ELIZABETH
*Location:* London
*Classification:* Unknown
*Date mark registered:* Unknown
*Active:* ca. 1746
*Marital status at registration:* Spinster (?)
*Source:* Pinchbeck, p. 293; Goldsmiths' Hall
Apprentice Register, vol. 7, p. 93
*Additional information:* Apprenticed to Ann
Jaquin.

*Name:* BICKERSTAFF, ISABELLA
*Location:* London
*Classification:* Unknown
*Date mark registered:* Unknown
*Active:* Apprenticeship—1773–80
*Marital status at registration:* Unknown
*Source:* Smith, p. 68
*Additional information:* Goldsmiths' Hall
Apprentice Register, vol. 8, p. 238 (1773).
Freed by service May 3, 1780.

*Name:* BING, MARGARET
*Location:* Ramsgate
*Classification:* Silversmith
*Other classifications:* Dealer in hardware
*Date mark registered:* Unknown
*Active:* ca. 1795
*Marital status at registration:* Unknown
*Source:* Sun Insurance 11937, vol. 10, p. 266
*Additional information:* Sun Insurance Policy No.
641741, registered July 2, 1795: on two
adjoining houses, utensils and stock worth
£150 in each.

*Name:* BINLEY, MARGARET*
*Alternative spellings:* Bingley
*Location:* London
*Classification:* Smallworker
*Other classifications:* Bucklemaker, buttonmaker,
goldsmith
*Date mark registered:* May 15, 1764
*Active:* 1764–ca. 1773
*Marital status at registration:* Widow
*Address:* Gutter Lane
*Husband's name:* Richard Binley
*Husband's classification:* Smallworker
*Source:* Grimwade, p. 441
*Additional information:* Both Richard and
Margaret Binley specialized in wine labels.
Found in the Parliamentary Report list of 1773.

*Name:* BIRD, REBEKAH
*Location:* London
*Classification:* Smallworker
*Date mark registered:* November 7, 1721
*Marital status at registration:* Unknown
*Address:* Star Court, Bread Street Hill
*Source:* Grimwade, p. 442

*Name:* BLAKE, SARAH*
*Alternative spellings:* Blane
*Location:* London
*Classification:* Spoonmaker
*Date mark registered:* June 15, 1809
*Active:* 1809–ca. 1823
*Marital status at registration:* Widow
*In partnership with:* John William Blake (son?)
*Address:* 16 Long Acre
*Husband's name:* John Blake
*Husband's classification:* Smallworker,
spoonmaker
*Source:* Grimwade, p. 442
*Additional information:* Second mark registered
January 9, 1821; third November 7, 1821.
John William Blake registered a mark alone in
February 1823, by which time Sarah Blake had
presumably retired or died.

*Name:* BLAND, ELIZABETH
*Alternative spellings:* Blane
*Location:* London
*Classification:* Silversmith
*Date mark registered:* September 16, 1794
*Active:* From 1791 (?)
*Marital status at registration:* Widow
*In partnership with:* James Huell Bland (son)
*Address:* 126 Bunhill Row
*Husband's name:* Cornelius Bland
*Husband's classification:* Silverchaser, plateworker
*Source:* Grimwade, p. 443

*Additional information:* The Gilbert Collection at the Los Angeles County Museum of Art has an astonishing, large cistern with royal arms bearing the mark of this partnership.

*Name:* BRAY, ISABELLA
*Location:* Westminster
*Classification:* Watchmaker
*Date mark registered:* Unknown
*Marital status at registration:* Wife
*In partnership with:* Thomas Bray (husband)
*Address:* 8 Little Queen Street
*Source:* Sun Insurance policies 1804, 1807, 1810
*Additional information:* The Brays worked in partnership with Ann and James Mahon; also Catherine and John Wright.

*Name:* BROOMHALL, ELIZABETH
*Location:* London
*Classification:* Watchmaker
*Date mark registered:* Unknown
*Active:* ca. 1810
*Marital status at registration:* Unknown
*In partnership with:* Robert Shearsmith
*Address:* 41 Stanhope Street, Clare Market
*Source:* Sun Insurance 11936, vol. 453, p. 1
*Additional information:* Sun Insurance Policy No. 850419, registered November 1, 1810: on household goods in dwelling house, wearing apparel, and plate £200, utensils and stock in trust £200.

*Name:* BROWN, ELIZABETH
*Location:* Coventry
*Classification:* Unknown
*Date mark registered:* Unknown
*Active:* 1822–25
*Marital status at registration:* Unknown
*In partnership with:* William Brown
*Address:* Well Street
*Source:* Grimwade, p. 720

*Name:* BURMAN, ANN
*Location:* London
*Classification:* Goldworker
*Date mark registered:* November 1, 1831
*Marital status at registration:* Unknown
*Address:* 1 Exeter Place, Dover Road, Southwark
*Source:* Grimwade, p. 355

*Name:* BURROWS, ALICE*
*Location:* London
*Classification:* Plateworker
*Date mark registered:* July 10, 1801 (two sizes)

*Active:* 1801–ca. 1819
*Marital status at registration:* Widow
*In partnership with:* George Burrows II (son)
*Address:* 14 Red Lion Street, Clerkenwell
*Husband's name:* George Burrows I
*Husband's classification:* Smallworker
*Source:* Grimwade, p. 454
*Additional information:* Second mark registered November 7, 1804; third February 21, 1810; fourth May 6, 1818. Retired or died by May 1819.

*Name:* BURROWS, ELIZABETH
*Location:* London
*Classification:* Silversmith
*Date mark registered:* Unknown
*Active:* ca. 1794
*Marital status at registration:* Unknown
*Address:* 104 Whitechapel Road
*Source:* Sun Insurance 11936, vol. 399
*Additional information:* Sun Insurance Policy No. 634280, registered October 29, 1794: on three houses in Shadwell High Street, one unspecified, one a butcher with slaughterhouse, the third a broker "warranted no cabinetmakers and carpenters work carried on or stove for drying feathers" £1,300 total.

*Name:* BUSFIELD, HANNAH
*Location:* York
*Classification:* Goldsmith
*Date mark registered:* Unknown
*Active:* ca. 1724
*Marital status at registration:* Unknown
*Address:* Coney Street, St. Martins
*Source:* Sun Insurance 11936, vol. 17, p. 527
*Additional information:* Sun Insurance Policy No. 32563, registered August 20, 1724: no total. John Busfield of York, goldsmith (son?) registered policy March 25, 1740.

*Name:* BUTEUX, ELIZABETH (see Godfrey, Elizabeth)

*Name:* BUTTALL, SARAH*
*Location:* London
*Classification:* Largeworker
*Date mark registered:* May 10, 1754
*Active:* 1754–ca. 1772
*Marital status at registration:* Unknown
*Address:* Minories
*Source:* Grimwade, p. 456

*Name:* CARMAN, MARY
*Location:* London
*Classification:* Smallworker
*Other classifications:* Hiltmaker

*Date mark registered:* January 20, 1764
*Marital status at registration:* Widow
*Address:* Holborn
*Husband's name:* John Carman II
*Husband's classification:* Cutler, working goldsmith
*Source:* Grimwade, p. 459
*Additional information:* Address of husband was the "Ewer and Swords," a reminder of the variety of goods manufactured and sold.

*Name:* CARPENTER, SARAH
*Location:* London
*Classification:* Casemaker
*Date mark registered:* August 3, 1791 (incuse mark)
*Marital status at registration:* Widow
*Address:* 9 Islington Road
*Husband's name:* Thomas Carpenter
*Husband's classification:* Casemaker
*Source:* Grimwade, p. 317

*Name:* CARTER, MARY
*Location:* London
*Classification:* Watchmaker
*Date mark registered:* Unknown
*Active:* ca. 1745
*Marital status at registration:* Widow
*Source:* Sun Insurance 11936, vol. 74, p. 287
*Additional information:* Sun Insurance Policy No. 103663, registered October 18, 1745: on dwelling house £700, apartments therein £100, wearing apparel £100.

*Name:* CHAMPION, ELEANOR
*Location:* Dublin
*Classification:* Jeweler
*Date mark registered:* Unknown
*Active:* Pre-1775–ca. 1792
*Marital status at registration:* Widow (?)
*In partnership with:* Keen at 3 College Green, 1780–83
*Address:* 30 Grafton Street to 1784; 3 College Green to 1792
*Husband's name:* James Champion (?)
*Husband's classification:* Jeweler (?)
*Source:* Bennett (1972), p. 300
*Additional information:* James Champion died in 1761.

*Name:* CHAWNER, MARY*
*Maiden name:* Burwash
*Location:* London
*Classification:* Spoonmaker
*Date mark registered:* April 14, 1834
*Marital status at registration:* Widow

*Address:* 16 Hosier Lane
*Husband's name:* William Chawner II
*Husband's classification:* Spoonmaker
*Source:* Grimwade, p. 463
*Additional information:* Five new marks March 25, 1835. She was the daughter of William Burwash, watchcase maker, and her brother William was apprenticed to her husband in 1816, the year of their marriage. William Chawner died March 20, 1834.

*Name:* CHESTERMAN, ANN
*Location:* London
*Classification:* Smallworker
*Date mark registered:* April 5, 1775
*Marital status at registration:* Widow
*Address:* Fleet Market
*Husband's name:* Charles Chesterman I
*Husband's classification:* Largeworker, goldsmith, pawnbroker
*Source:* Grimwade, p. 464
*Additional information:* Ann Chesterman had died by April 5, 1780, when her apprentice, Samuel Wheatley, was turned over to Charles Chesterman II by her executor, Sarah Chesterman.

*Name:* CLARK, MARTHA
*Location:* London
*Classification:* Watchcase maker
*Date mark registered:* April 25, 1805 (incuse mark)
*Marital status at registration:* Unknown
*In partnership with:* Joseph Clark (son?)
*Address:* 70 Bunhill Row
*Source:* Sun Insurance policies; Grimwade, p. 313
*Additional information:* Sun Insurance Policy, registered October 5, 1802: on adjoining houses £1,000 total. Sun Insurance Policy, registered January 24, 1807: on house £450, apparel and plate £400, utensils and stock including plate £200, two rooms behind rear £50, No. 71 in tenure of a dealer in skins £500. Joseph Clark was watchcase maker entered at 71 Bunhill Row.

*Name:* CLARK, SARAH
*Location:* Birmingham
*Classification:* Unknown
*Date mark registered:* Unknown
*Active:* ca. 1842
*Marital status at registration:* Widow (?)
*Address:* 52 Lionel Street (?)
*Husband's name:* Francis Clark (?)
*Husband's classification:* Plateworker (?)
*Source:* Smith, p. 69

*Additional information:* Francis Clark was active
*ca.* 1826.


*Name:* CLARKE, CATHERINE
*Location:* London
*Classification:* Smallworker
*Other classifications:* Goldsmith
*Date mark registered:* September 24, 1761
*Active:* 1761–*ca.* 1774
*Marital status at registration:* Unknown
*Address:* Dorset Court; Salisbury Court;
Fleet Street
*Source:* Grimwade, p. 465


*Name:* CLARKE, SARAH
*Location:* London
*Classification:* Smallworker
*Other classifications:* Bucklemaker, goldsmith
*Date mark registered:* April 22, 1765
*Active:* 1765–*ca.* 1777
*Marital status at registration:* Unknown
*Address:* In the Borough of Southwark
*Source:* Grimwade, p. 466
*Additional information:* She married Crispin
Fuller, the apprentice of her grandmother
Hester Bateman.


*Name:* CLAYTON, RUTH
*Location:* London
*Classification:* Smallworker
*Date mark registered:* December 31, 1697
*Marital status at registration:* Unknown
*Address:* Ball Alley, Lombard Street
*Source:* Grimwade, p. 467


*Name:* CLERKE, SARAH
*Location:* London
*Classification:* Watchcase maker
*Date mark registered:* January 11, 1813
*Marital status at registration:* Unknown
*Address:* 23 Banner Square
*Source:* Grimwade, p. 318
*Additional information:* Second mark registered
July 29, 1813.


*Name:* COLLIER, ELIZA
*Alternative spellings:* Elizabeth (?)
*Location:* Dublin
*Classification:* Button manufacturer
*Date mark registered:* Unknown
*Active:* 1813–*ca.* 1817
*Marital status at registration:* Unknown
*In partnership with:* Michael Murphy Collier
*Address:* 110 Bride Street
*Source:* Bennett (1972), p. 320


*Name:* COOKE, ELIZABETH*
*Location:* London
*Classification:* Smallworker
*Other classifications:* Silversmith
*Date mark registered:* January 24, 1764
*Marital status at registration:* Widow
*Address:* Foster Lane
*Husband's name:* Thomas Cooke II
*Husband's classification:* Largeworker
*Source:* Grimwade, p. 470
*Additional information:* Thomas Cooke II died in
1761.


*Name:* COOKE, ELIZABETH
*Location:* Birmingham
*Classification:* Goldworker
*Date mark registered:* 1792
*Marital status at registration:* Unknown
*Address:* "town"
*Source:* Grimwade, p. 717


*Name:* COOKE, SARAH
*Location:* London
*Classification:* Unknown
*Date mark registered:* Unknown
*Active:* Apprenticeship—1736–47
*Marital status at registration:* Unknown
*Source:* Smith, p. 68
*Additional information:* Goldsmiths' Hall
Apprentice Register, vol. 6, p. 225 (1736).
Freed by service September 16, 1747.


*Name:* CORMICK, ANN
*Location:* Dublin
*Classification:* Goldbeater
*Other classifications:* Goldsmith, jeweler, lace
manufacturer, refiner
*Date mark registered:* Unknown
*Active:* 1780–*ca.* 1802
*Marital status at registration:* Unknown
*In partnership with:* John Cormick
*Address:* 22 Parliament Street
*Husband's name:* Michael Cormick
*Source:* Bennett (1972), p. 301
*Additional information:* Michael Cormick died in
1780. Ann Cormick's partnership with John
Cormick extended from 1789 to *ca.* 1799.


*Name:* CORRY, MARY
*Location:* London
*Classification:* Smallworker
*Date mark registered:* April 21, 1768
*Marital status at registration:* Widow
*Address:* Aldergate Street
*Husband's name:* Henry Corry

*Husband's classification:* Largeworker
*Source:* Grimwade, p. 473

*Name:* COURTAULD, LOUISA PERINA*
*Maiden name:* Ogier
*Alternative spellings:* Onger
*Location:* London
*Classification:* Goldsmith
*Other classifications:* Jeweler
*Date mark registered: ca.* 1765 (Register missing)
*Active: ca.* 1765–*ca.* 1780
*Marital status at registration:* Wife (?)
*In partnership with:* 1) Samuel Courtauld I (husband), *ca.* 1765; 2) George Cowles, *ca.* 1768–77; 3) Samuel Courtauld II (son), 1777–80
*Address:* Crown, 21 Cornhill
*Husband's name:* Samuel Courtauld I
*Husband's classification:* Largeworker
*Source:* Grimwade, p. 474
*Additional information:* Louisa Courtauld's first mark was entered with her husband; the museum's collection includes a pair of urn-shaped tea caddies from 1766 with their joint mark. Second mark, with George Cowles, registered *ca.* 1768; third mark, with Samuel Courtauld II, October 16, 1777. Louisa and Samuel Courtauld I were married August 31, 1749. He died in February 1765. She died January 12, 1807.

*Name:* CRAIG, ANN*
*Location:* London
*Classification:* Largeworker
*Date mark registered:* October 15, 1740
*Active:* 1740–*ca.* 1745
*Marital status at registration:* Widow
*In partnership with:* John Neville
*Address:* Corner of Norris Street, St. James's, Haymarket
*Husband's name:* John Craig
*Husband's classification:* Silversmith
*Source:* Grimwade, p. 477
*Additional information:* Second mark registered May 27, 1743. Her husband was in partnership with George Wickes *ca.* 1730–35 at same address. Her brother (?) David Craig was apprenticed to George Wickes in 1731. John Craig died *ca.* 1735.

*Name:* CRAMMILLION, HANNAH
*Alternative spellings:* Cromillou (?)
*Location:* London
*Classification:* Watchcase maker
*Other classifications:* Smallworker
*Date mark registered:* February 8, 1762

*Active:* 1762–*ca.* 1773
*Marital status at registration:* Widow
*In partnership with:* Peter Crammillion II (son)
*Address:* Clerkenwell Green
*Husband's name:* Peter Crammillion I
*Husband's classification:* Casemaker (?)
*Source:* Grimwade, p. 477
*Additional information:* Peter Crammillion II was turned over to his mother April 4, 1754, to serve his apprenticeship. Peter Crammillion I died before April 1754.

*Name:* CRAWFORD, SARAH
*Location:* Newcastle upon Tyne
*Classification:* Silversmith
*Date mark registered:* 1796
*Active:* 1796–*ca.* 1798
*Marital status at registration:* Widow
*Husband's name:* James Crawford
*Husband's classification:* Silversmith
*Source:* Gill, p. 86
*Additional information:* James Crawford died in May 1795.

*Name:* CROSWELL, MARY ANN*
*Location:* London
*Classification:* Smallworker
*Date mark registered:* May 21, 1805
*Active:* 1805–*ca.* 1819, perhaps to 1830
*Marital status at registration:* Widow
*Address:* 31 Monkwell Street
*Husband's name:* Henry Croswell I
*Husband's classification:* Smallworker
*Source:* Grimwade, p. 480
*Additional information:* Second mark registered August 29, 1816. Her son Henry Croswell was apprenticed to her in October 1819.

*Name:* CUMMINS, ANN
*Location:* Dublin
*Classification:* Unknown
*Date mark registered:* 1848–*ca.* 1855
*Marital status at registration:* Unknown
*Address:* Harolds Cross
*Source:* Bennett (1984), p. 141

*Name:* CUNY, ELIZABETH
*Alternative spellings:* Cugny, de Cuney; misspelling Curry
*Location:* London
*Classification:* Goldsmith
*Date mark registered:* Unknown
*Active: ca.* 1733–*ca.* 1738
*Marital status at registration:* Widow
*In partnership with:* Henry Hebert (?)
*Address:* Spur Street, Leicester Fields

*Husband's name:* Louis Cuny
*Husband's classification:* Goldsmith
*Source:* Grimwade, p. 482; Sun Insurance policies
*Additional information:* Sun Insurance Policy No. 62791, registered January 14, 1733: on goods, utensils, stock, and manufactured plate £500. Sun Insurance Policy No. 79087, registered December 22, 1738: £500 total. Louis Cuny died in December 1733

*Name:* DALRYMPLE, HANNAH
*Location:* Dublin
*Classification:* Unknown
*Date mark registered:* Unknown
*Active:* ca. 1780–ca. 1783
*Marital status at registration:* Widow
*Address:* 42 Aungier Street
*Husband's name:* John Dalrymple I
*Husband's classification:* Watchmaker
*Source:* Bennett (1972), p. 303
*Additional information:* John Dalrymple died in 1779.

*Name:* DANIEL, JANE
*Alternative spellings:* Daniell, Dancell
*Location:* Dublin
*Classification:* Unknown
*Date mark registered:* Unknown
*Active:* ca. 1740
*Marital status at registration:* Widow
*Husband's name:* Henry Daniel
*Source:* Bennett (1972), p. 303; Smith, p. 69
*Additional information:* Henry Daniel was apprenticed to Thomas Bolton in 1703. He died in 1737. Jane Daniel used her husband's mark.

*Name:* DARE, ELLEN
*Maiden name:* Knight
*Location:* Taunton
*Classification:* Unknown
*Date mark registered:* Unknown
*Active:* 1680–ca. 1739
*Marital status at registration:* Widow
*Husband's name:* Thomas Dare
*Husband's classification:* Goldsmith
*Source:* Kent research
*Additional information:* Used Thomas Dare's mark and subsequently her own cinquefoil. Appears to have subcontracted work to other Taunton silversmiths, such as Samuel Dell and Richard Hamlin. Ellen Dare presumably worked with her two younger sons, John and James. Thomas Dare died in 1685. Ellen Dare died in 1739.

*Name:* DAVENPORT, SARAH
*Location:* London
*Classification:* Smallworker
*Date mark registered:* 1813
*Marital status at registration:* Widow
*Husband's name:* Samuel Davenport
*Husband's classification:* Plateworker, smallworker
*Source:* Grimwade, p. 485

*Name:* DAWSON, ELIZABETH
*Location:* London
*Classification:* Casemaker
*Date mark registered:* June 22, 1778 (incuse mark)
*Marital status at registration:* Widow
*Address:* Oxford Arms Passage, Warwick Lane
*Husband's name:* William Dawson
*Husband's classification:* Smallworker, watchcase maker
*Source:* Grimwade, p. 486
*Additional information:* William Dawson, a casemaker whose incuse mark is recorded in 1781 and 1786, may be Elizabeth Dawson's son.

*Name:* DEAN, ELIZABETH
*Location:* London
*Classification:* Unknown
*Date mark registered:* Unknown
*Active:* Apprenticeship—1670–79
*Marital status at registration:* Unknown
*Source:* Smith, p. 68
*Additional information:* Goldsmiths' Hall Apprentice Register, vol. 2, p. 189 (1670). Freed by service July 16, 1679.

*Name:* DEARDS, MARY
*Alternative spellings:* Deard, Marie
*Location:* London
*Classification:* Goldsmith
*Other classifications:* Toyman
*Date mark registered:* Unknown
*Active:* after 1765
*Marital status at registration:* Unknown
*In partnership with:* William Deards
*Address:* The Star, end of Pall Mall
*Source:* Grimwade, p. 487; Heal, p. 138
*Additional information:* Bilingual trade card "William & Mary Deards/Guillaume et Marie Deards" in Heal.

*Name:* DEARMER, MARY
*Location:* London
*Classification:* Casemaker (incuse mark)
*Date mark registered:* February 12, 1798

*Marital status at registration:* Unknown
*Address:* 14 Featherstone Street, Bunhill
*Source:* Grimwade, p. 313

*Name:* DELL, SUSANNA
*Alternative spellings:* Deale
*Location:* Taunton
*Classification:* Unknown
*Date mark registered:* Unknown
*Active: ca.* 1698
*Marital status at registration:* Widow
*Husband's name:* Samuel Dell
*Husband's classification:* Goldsmith
*Source:* Kent research
*Additional information:* Samuel Dell died in
1698.

*Name:* DENTON, MARY
*Location:* Oxford
*Classification:* Clock and watchmaker
*Other classifications:* Dealer in hardware
*Date mark registered:* Unknown
*Active: ca.* 1798
*Marital status at registration:* Unknown
*Address:* High Street
*Source:* Sun Insurance 11937, vol. 22, p. 544
*Additional information:* Sun Insurance Policy No.
676755, registered April 4, 1798: on household
goods in dwelling house £50, utensils and
stock goods in trust (plate included) £50,
dwelling house £200.

*Name:* DESVIGNES, ANN
*Maiden name:* Macaire
*Alternative spellings:* Desvigny
*Location:* London
*Classification:* Goldworker
*Date mark registered:* October 5, 1813
*Active:* 1793–ca. 1813
*Marital status at registration:* Widow
*Address:* 44 Rosoman Street, Clerkenwell
*Husband's name:* Peter Desvignes
*Husband's classification:* Goldworker
*Source:* Grimwade, p. 491
*Additional information:* Earlier incuse mark as
Ann Macaire and Peter Desvignes registered
November 11, 1793. Former address 13
Denmark Street, Soho.

*Name:* DORRELL, JANE
*Location:* London
*Classification:* Smallworker
*Other classifications:* Buttonmaker, plateworker
*Date mark registered:* October 22, 1766
*Active:* 1766–ca. 1781
*Marital status at registration:* Widow

*In partnership with:* Richard May (former
apprentice of William Dorrell)
*Address:* 24 Quakers' Buildings, Smithfield
*Husband's name:* William Dorrell
*Husband's classification:* Smallworker
*Source:* Grimwade, p. 493
*Additional information:* Second mark registered
May 22, 1769; third May 3, 1771. Jane Dorrell
appears alone as a buttonmaker in the
Parliamentary Report of 1773. Heal records the
partnership as plateworkers from 1771 to 1781.

*Name:* DOWTHWAITE, SUSANNA
*Alternative spellings:* Dowthett
*Location:* Newcastle upon Tyne
*Classification:* Goldsmith
*Date mark registered:* Unknown
*Active: ca.* 1673–ca. 1676
*Marital status at registration:* Widow
*Address:* All Saints
*Husband's name:* John Dowthwaite
*Husband's classification:* Goldsmith
*Source:* Gill, p. 97
*Additional information:* John Dowthwaite died in
1673. Susanna Dowthwaite carried on the
business until 1676, and then married Francis
Batty, her husband's former apprentice.

*Name:* DUNNE, MARY
*Location:* Dublin
*Classification:* Goldsmith
*Date mark registered:* 1784
*Marital status at registration:* Unknown
*Address:* 10 Christchurch Yard
*Source:* Bennett (1972), p. 304

*Name:* EASTWICK, HENRIETTA
*Location:* London
*Classification:* Smallworker
*Date mark registered:* June 26, 1782
*Active:* 1782–ca. 1802
*Marital status at registration:* Widow
*Address:* 102 Aldersgate Street
*Husband's name:* Adrian Eastwick
*Husband's classification:* Smallworker
*Source:* Grimwade, p. 499
*Additional information:* Second mark registered
September 12, 1789; third, in partnership with
William Eastwick (son?), September 11, 1802.

*Name:* EATON, ELIZABETH*
*Location:* London
*Classification:* Manufacturing silversmith
*Date mark registered:* 1845
*Active:* 1845–ca. 1854
*Marital status at registration:* Widow

*Address:* 16 Jewin Crescent, Aldersgate, St.
Cripplegate
*Husband's name:* William Eaton
*Husband's classification:* Manufacturing
silversmith
*Source:* Culme, p. 134
*Additional information:* Second mark, in
partnership with John Eaton (son), registered
1854. Exhibited at Great Exhibition 1851.
William Eaton died in 1845.

*Name:* ELVIE, MRS.
*Location:* Dartmouth
*Classification:* Silversmith
*Date mark registered:* Unknown
*Active:* ca. 1699
*Marital status at registration:* Widow
*Husband's name:* Peter Elvie
*Husband's classification:* Silversmith
*Source:* Kent research

*Name:* EMES, REBECCA*
*Alternative spellings:* Rebeccah
*Location:* London
*Classification:* Plateworker
*Date mark registered:* June 30, 1808
*Active:* 1808–ca. 1829
*Marital status at registration:* Widow
*In partnership with:* 1) William Emes (possible
brother-in-law), 1808; 2) Edward Barnard,
1808–ca. 1829
*Address:* Amen Corner
*Husband's name:* John Emes
*Husband's classification:* Goldsmith
*Source:* Grimwade, p. 504
*Additional information:* The partnership of Emes
and Barnard ran one of the largest silver
workshops of the period. Among the retailers
they supplied were the London firm of
Rundell, Bridge & Rundell and Cattle &
Barber in York. Second mark registered in
partnership with Edward Barnard October 14,
1808; third April 29, 1818; fourth February 20,
1821; fifth October 29, 1825. William Emes,
who may have been Rebecca Emes's brother-
in-law, was executor of John Emes's estate.
Edward Barnard entered a mark with his two
sons on February 25, 1829, by which time
Rebecca Emes had presumably retired or died.

*Name:* ENTWHISTLE, MARY
*Location:* London
*Classification:* Unknown
*Date mark registered:* Unknown
*Active:* Apprenticeship—1719–28
*Marital status at registration:* Unknown

*Source:* Smith, p. 68
*Additional information:* Goldsmiths' Hall
Apprentice Register, vol. 5, p. 99 (1719).
Freed by service March 5, 1728.

*Name:* EUSTACE, ELIZABETH
*Location:* Exeter
*Classification:* Unknown
*Date mark registered:* Unknown
*Active:* ca. 1789–ca. 1796
*Marital status at registration:* Unknown
*Husband's name:* Thomas Eustace
*Source:* Kent research
*Additional information:* After Thomas Eustace's
bankruptcy in 1789, Elizabeth Eustace
presumably ran the business. She is listed in an
Exeter directory of 1796.

*Name:* FARREN, ANN
*Alternative spellings:* Farrar, Farrer
*Location:* London
*Classification:* Largeworker
*Date mark registered:* October 19, 1743
*Marital status at registration:* Widow
*Address:* St. Swithin's Lane
*Husband's name:* Thomas Farren
*Husband's classification:* Largeworker
*Source:* Grimwade, p. 506
*Additional information:* Grimwade, p. 732:
"[Thomas Farren's] will proved 21 October
1743: 'unto my dear and loving wife Ann
Farren all my ready monies, stock in trade,
plate, goods, Chatells . . . and all other
personal estate whatsoever,' she as sole executrix
(Information from Mr. T. Kent)."

*Name:* FAWDERY, HESTER
*Location:* London
*Classification:* Largeworker
*Date mark registered:* September 28, 1727
*Marital status at registration:* Widow
*Address:* Goldsmith Street, near Cheapside
*Husband's name:* William Fawdery
*Husband's classification:* Largeworker
*Source:* Grimwade, p. 507

*Name:* FELINE, MAGDALEN*
*Alternative spellings:* Fellen, Pheline
*Location:* London
*Classification:* Largeworker
*Other classifications:* Plateworker
*Date mark registered:* May 15, 1753
*Active:* 1753–ca. 1762
*Marital status at registration:* Widow
*Address:* King Street, Covent Garden
*Husband's name:* Edward Feline

*Husband's classification:* Largeworker
*Source:* Grimwade, p. 508
*Additional information:* Second mark registered
January 18, 1757. Edward Feline was
apprenticed to Augustine Courtauld in 1709.


*Name:* FENNEL, EDITH
*Location:* London
*Classification:* Unknown
*Date mark registered:* Unknown
*Active:* ca. 1780
*Marital status at registration:* Unknown
*Source:* Smith, p. 69


*Name:* FIELD, MARY
*Location:* Gloucester
*Classification:* Goldsmith
*Date mark registered:* Unknown
*Active:* ca. 1745
*Marital status at registration:* Widow
*Address:* St. Michael's Parish
*Source:* Sun Insurance 11936, vol. 74, p. 422
*Additional information:* Sun Insurance Policy No.
104040, registered December 23, 1745.


*Name:* FLEMING, ANN
*Location:* Waterford, County Waterford
*Classification:* Unknown
*Date mark registered:* 1784
*Marital status at registration:* Unknown
*Address:* Corner of Broad Street and the Square
*Source:* Bennett (1972), p. 352
*Additional information:* Registered in Dublin.


*Name:* FLETCHER, ANN
*Location:* London
*Classification:* Smallworker
*Other classifications:* Free clockmaker
*Date mark registered:* Undated, presumably
April 1697 on commencement of Register
*Marital status at registration:* Unknown
*Address:* St. Martin's Le Grand
*Source:* Grimwade, p. 510
*Additional information:* Probably free by
patrimony.


*Name:* FLETCHER, EDITH
*Location:* London
*Classification:* Largeworker
*Date mark registered:* Undated, between
February 1729 and January 1732
*Marital status at registration:* Widow
*Address:* Foster Lane
*Source:* Grimwade, p. 510

*Name:* FLETCHER, ELIZABETH
*Location:* London
*Classification:* Unknown
*Date mark registered:* Unknown
*Active:* ca. 1727
*Marital status at registration:* Unknown
*Source:* Smith, p. 69


*Name:* FOOTE, ANN
*Location:* London
*Classification:* Unknown
*Date mark registered:* Unknown
*Active:* 1752
*Marital status at registration:* Widow (?)
*Husband's name:* John Foote (?)
*Source:* Wenham, p. 63
*Additional information:* Trade card illustrated in
Heal—"At the Ring near the Maypole
Eastsmithfield . . . Sells all Sorts of Goldsmiths
Work . . . Jewellers Work done at Home."


*Name:* FORBES, ESTHER
*Location:* Dublin
*Classification:* Unknown
*Date mark registered:* Unknown
*Active:* 1718–29
*Marital status at registration:* Widow
*Husband's name:* Robert Forbes
*Husband's classification:* Silversmith
*Source:* Bennett (1984), p. 143
*Additional information:* Registered three marks.


*Name:* FOSTER, ELIZABETH
*Location:* London
*Classification:* Goldworker
*Date mark registered:* May 2, 1801
*Marital status at registration:* Unknown
*Address:* 1 Bartlett Passage, Holborn
*Source:* Grimwade, p. 358


*Name:* FOSTER, HANNAH
*Location:* London
*Classification:* Hiltmaker
*Date mark registered:* June 10, 1795
*Marital status at registration:* Widow
*Address:* King's Head Court, Fetter Lane
*Husband's name:* John Foster II
*Husband's classification:* Smallworker
*Source:* Grimwade, p. 512


*Name:* FOSTER, MARY
*Location:* London
*Classification:* Unknown
*Date mark registered:* Unknown
*Active:* ca. 1734

*Marital status at registration:* Widow (?)
*Address:* 16 King's Head Court, Fetter Lane
*Husband's name:* Thomas Foster (?)
*Source:* Grimwade, pp. 512–13
*Additional information:* Son Thomas Foster was apprenticed to Josiah Daniel on December 3, 1734, and turned over the same day to his mother, Mary Foster.

*Name:* FOWLER, MARY ANN
*Location:* Exeter
*Classification:* Jeweler
*Date mark registered:* Unknown
*Active:* ca. 1830
*Marital status at registration:* Unknown
*Address:* Bampfylde Street
*Husband's name:* John Fowler (?)
*Source:* Kent research
*Additional information:* Her mark is found on an Exeter copperplate of the period.

*Name:* FOX, CATHERINE
*Location:* Dublin
*Classification:* Unknown
*Date mark registered:* 1784
*Active:* 1747–85
*Marital status at registration:* Wife or widow (?)
*Address:* 3 Parliament Street, East Side
*Source:* Bennett (1984), p. 143.

*Name:* FOX, SARAH
*Location:* Chatham
*Classification:* Goldsmith
*Date mark registered:* Unknown
*Active:* ca. 1671
*Marital status at registration:* Unknown
*Source:* Sun Insurance 11936, vol. 137, p. 59
*Additional information:* Sun Insurance Policy No. 180749, registered February 16, 1671.

*Name:* FRAILLON, BLANCHE
*Alternative spellings:* Ffailion, Blance
*Location:* London
*Classification:* Largeworker
*Date mark registered:* Undated, between September 1727 and June 1728
*Marital status at registration:* Widow
*Address:* Lanchester Court, The Strand
*Husband's name:* James Fraillon
*Husband's classification:* Largeworker
*Source:* Grimwade, p. 514

*Name:* FRANCE, ELIZABETH
*Location:* Manchester
*Classification:* Unknown
*Date mark registered:* Unknown

*Active:* ca. 1819
*Marital status at registration:* Unknown
*Source:* Smith, p. 69
*Additional information:* Registered in Chester.

*Name:* FRENCH, ANN
*Location:* Chester
*Classification:* Unknown
*Date mark registered:* Unknown
*Active:* ca. 1819
*Marital status at registration:* Unknown
*Source:* Valentine manuscript

*Name:* FRENCH, ANN and ELIZABETH
*Location:* Birmingham
*Classification:* Silvercasters
*Date mark registered:* Unknown
*Active:* ca. 1818–ca. 1821
*Marital status at registration:* Unknown
*In partnership with:* 1) William Jones; 2) William Jones and William Jennings
*Source:* Smith, p. 81
*Additional information:* They worked in partnership with William Jennings in 1821. Ann and Elizabeth may have been sisters.

*Name:* FRY, ELIZABETH
*Location:* London
*Classification:* Goldworker
*Date mark registered:* December 6, 1775
*Marital status at registration:* Widow (?)
*Address:* 6 Bull and Mouth Street
*Husband's name:* John Fry I (?)
*Husband's classification:* Smallworker (?)
*Source:* Grimwade, pp. 358, 516

*Name:* FULLER, ANN
*Location:* Birmingham
*Classification:* Unknown
*Date mark registered:* Unknown
*Active:* ca. 1809
*Marital status at registration:* Unknown
*Source:* Smith, p. 69

*Name:* GALLANT, JANE
*Location:* London
*Classification:* Smallworker
*Other classifications:* Watchcase maker
*Date mark registered:* May 25, 1760
*Active:* 1760–ca. 1773
*Marital status at registration:* Unknown
*Address:* Smarts Building, Holborn
*Source:* Grimwade, p. 517
*Additional information:* Appears as watchcase maker in Parliamentary Report of 1773.

*Name:* GAMMON, MARIA
*Location:* Hereford
*Classification:* Silversmith
*Other classifications:* Watchmaker
*Date mark registered:* Unknown
*Active:* ca. 1786
*Marital status at registration:* Unknown
*Address:* Market Place
*Source:* Sun Insurance 11936, vol. 339, p. 131
*Additional information:* Sun Insurance Policy No.
520557, registered July 22, 1786: on dwelling
house £200, utensils and stock £800.

*Name:* GAMON, DINAH*
*Location:* London
*Classification:* Largeworker
*Date mark registered:* March 6, 1740
*Marital status at registration:* Widow
*Address:* Staining Lane, near Goldsmiths' Hall
*Husband's name:* John Gamon
*Husband's classification:* Largeworker
*Source:* Grimwade, p. 518
*Additional information:* Dinah and John Gamon
had two sons, William (born 1728) and John
(born 1730). The latter was apprenticed to
John Ruffin of the Goldsmiths' Company.

*Name:* GIBBS, ELIZABETH
*Location:* London
*Classification:* Unknown
*Date mark registered:* Unknown
*Active:* Apprenticeship—1667–95
*Marital status at registration:* Unknown
*Source:* Smith, p. 68
*Additional information:* Goldsmiths' Hall
Apprentice Register, vol. 2, p. 162 (1667).
Freed by service November 27, 1695.

*Name:* GIBSON, MRS.
*Location:* London
*Classification:* Silversmith
*Date mark registered:* Unknown
*Active:* ca. 1755
*Marital status at registration:* Widow (?)
*Address:* Bishopsgate Street
*Source:* Grimwade, p. 521
*Additional information:* Perhaps daughter-in-law
of Edward Gibson.

*Name:* GILL, JANE
*Location:* London
*Classification:* Goldworker
*Date mark registered:* February 5, 1834
*Marital status at registration:* Unknown
*Address:* 10 Lower Smith Street, Northampton
Square
*Source:* Grimwade, p. 371

*Name:* GLOVER, ANN
*Location:* London
*Classification:* Goldworker
*Date mark registered:* October 2, 1809
*Marital status at registration:* Unknown
*Address:* 4 Noble Street
*Source:* Grimwade, p. 355

*Name:* GLOVER, SARAH
*Location:* London
*Classification:* Goldworker
*Date mark registered:* July 1, 1822
*Marital status at registration:* Widow (?)
*Address:* 4 Bull and Mouth Street
*Husband's name:* Samuel Glover (?)
*Husband's classification:* Goldworker (?)
*Source:* Grimwade, p. 378

*Name:* GODFREY, ELIZABETH*
*Maiden name:* Pantin
*Alternative spellings:* Pentin, Eliza
*First married name:* Buteux
*Alternative spellings:* Bettew, Elisabeth
*Location:* London
*Classification:* Goldsmith
*Other classifications:* Silversmith, jeweler,
largeworker
*Date mark registered:* November 15, 1731
*Active:* 1731–ca. 1758
*Marital status at registration:* Widow
*Address:* Norris Street, Haymarket
*Husband's name:* Benjamin Godfrey
*Husband's classification:* Largeworker
*Source:* Grimwade, pp. 456, 524
*Additional information:* First married to Abraham
Buteux, February 11, 1720. Abraham Buteux
presumably died by 1731, when she registered
her first mark as Elizabeth Buteux. She carried
on the business as a widow until her marriage
to Benjamin Godfrey, her journeyman, October
3, 1732. Second mark, as Elizabeth Godfrey,
registered June 29, 1741, presumably on
Benjamin Godfrey's death.

*Name:* GODLEY, MARY
*Location:* London
*Classification:* Silver flatter
*Date mark registered:* Unknown
*Active:* ca. 1777
*Marital status at registration:* Widow
*Address:* Bagnio Court, 18 Aldersgate Street
*Husband's name:* Benjamin Godley
*Source:* Sun Insurance 11936, vol. 258, p. 624
*Additional information:* Sun Insurance Policy No.
388501, registered September 11, 1777: £1,000
total. Moved from Bagnio Court 1776.

Name: GOODWIN, ELIZABETH
Location: London
Classification: Largeworker
Date mark registered: December 2, 1729
Marital status at registration: Widow
Address: Noble Street
Husband's name: James Goodwin
Husband's classification: Working goldsmith
Source: Grimwade, p. 525
Additional information: John Spackman II was apprenticed to her October 21, 1730.

Name: GOULD, MARY*
Alternative spellings: Mrs. James Gould
Location: London
Classification: Largeworker
Date mark registered: August 31, 1747
Marital status at registration: Widow
Address: Golden Bottle, Ave Maria Lane
Husband's name: James Gould
Husband's classification: Candlestick maker
Source: Grimwade, pp. 526–27
Additional information: Mary Gould used her husband's IG mark.

Name: GOVETT, SARAH
Location: London
Classification: Watchcase maker
Date mark registered: December 2, 1823
Marital status at registration: Widow
Address: 47 Ironmongers Row, St. Luke's
Husband's name: Matthew Govett
Source: Grimwade, p. 348

Name: GRANT, DOROTHY
Alternative spellings: Graunt
Location: London
Classification: Largeworker
Date mark registered: Undated, probably 1697 on commencement of the Register
Marital status at registration: Widow
Address: In the Borough of Southwark
Husband's name: William Grant
Husband's classification: Goldsmith
Source: Grimwade, p. 527

Name: GRAY, ANN
Location: London
Classification: Goldsmith
Other classifications: Toyman, cutler
Date mark registered: Unknown
Marital status at registration: Unknown
In partnership with: William Gray
Address: New Bond Street
Source: Sun Insurance 11936, vol. 373
Additional information: Sun Insurance Policy No. 581976, registered April 8, 1791: £3,500 total.

Name: GREAME, ANN
Location: London
Classification: Unknown
Date mark registered: Unknown
Active: Apprenticeship—1736–59
Marital status at registration: Unknown
Source: Smith, p. 68
Additional information: Goldsmiths' Hall Apprentice Register, vol. 6, p. 230 (1736). Freed by service October 5, 1759.

Name: GREAME, ELIZABETH
Location: London
Classification: Unknown
Date mark registered: Unknown
Active: Apprenticeship—1762–71
Marital status at registration: Unknown
Source: Smith, p. 68
Additional information: Goldsmiths' Hall Apprentice Register, vol, 7, p. 331 (1762). Freed by service January 9, 1771.

Name: GREGOR, ANN
Location: London
Classification: Unknown
Date mark registered: Unknown
Active: Apprenticeship—1684–1701
Marital status at registration: Unknown
Source: Smith, p. 68
Additional information: Goldsmiths' Hall Apprentice Register, vol. 3, p. 135 (1684). Freed by service November 21, 1701.

Name: GROVE, ANN
Location: London
Classification: Casemaker
Date mark registered: December 20, 1813
Marital status at registration: Unknown
In partnership with: James Melville
Address: 9 Vineyard Walk
Source: Grimwade, p. 288
Additional information: Second mark, alone, registered September 12, 1814, at 2 Vineyard Walk.

Name: HAMMOND, ELIZABETH
Location: London
Classification: Unknown
Date mark registered: Unknown
Active: Apprenticeship—1712–20
Marital status at registration: Unknown
Source: Smith, p. 68
Additional information: Goldsmiths' Hall Apprentice Register, vol. 5, p. 36 (1712). Freed by service July 7, 1720.

*Name:* HANSON, MARY
*Location:* Birmingham
*Classification:* Unknown
*Date mark registered:* 1811
*Active:* ca. 1811
*Marital status at registration:* Unknown
*Source:* Jackson, p. 367

*Name:* HARRIS, CATHERINE
*Location:* Maidstone, Kent
*Classification:* Goldsmith
*Date mark registered:* Unknown
*Active:* ca. 1744
*Marital status at registration:* Unknown
*Address:* High Street
*Source:* Sun Insurance 11936, vol. 73, p. 94
*Additional information:* Sun Insurance Policy No.
101228, registered January 11, 1744: on stock
or wrought manufactured plate included in
dwelling house £200, goods in trust (wrought
manufactured plate included) £150, wearing
apparel £50.

*Name:* HARRISON, MARGARET
*Location:* London
*Classification:* Smallworker
*Date mark registered:* January 21, 1764
*Active:* 1764–ca. 1773
*Marital status at registration:* Widow
*Address:* Lamb Court, Clerkenwell Green
*Husband's name:* Thomas Harrison
*Husband's classification:* Smallworker
*Source:* Grimwade, p. 538
*Additional information:* Second mark registered
March 19, 1764, at Shrift (Frith?) Street, Soho.

*Name:* HARTLEY, ELIZABETH
*Location:* London
*Classification:* Largeworker
*Date mark registered:* June 6, 1748
*Marital status at registration:* Widow (?)
*Address:* Mays Buildings
*Husband's name:* John Hartley (?)
*Source:* Grimwade, p. 539
*Additional information:* Moved to Maiden Lane,
Covent Garden, as of January 20, 1752 (?).

*Name:* HARTWELL, ELIZABETH
*Location:* Oxeter, Staffordshire
*Classification:* Clockmaker
*Other classifications:* Watchmaker
*Date mark registered:* Unknown
*Active:* ca. 1795
*Marital status at registration:* Unknown
*Source:* Sun Insurance 11937, vol. 9, p. 545
*Additional information:* Sun Insurance Policy No.

644891, registered September 3, 1795: on house
£100, wearing apparel £50, utensils and stock
£200.

*Name:* HARVEY, ANNE
*Alternative spellings:* Ann
*Location:* London
*Classification:* Smallworker
*Date mark registered:* Undated, between
February and March 1759
*Marital status at registration:* Single woman (?)
*In partnership with:* John Harvey II (brother?)
*Address:* Crown in Bear Lane, near
Christchurch in Surrey
*Source:* Grimwade, p. 539
*Additional information:* Born August 13, 1739 (?).

*Name:* HASELWOOD, ELIZABETH*
*Location:* Norwich
*Classification:* Unknown
*Date mark registered:* Unknown
*Active:* ca. 1685–1715
*Marital status at registration:* Widow
*Husband's name:* Arthur Haselwood II
*Source:* Barrett, p. 87
*Additional information:* Probably employed
journeymen goldsmiths. Left shop to her son
Arthur Haselwood III. Died in 1715 at the
age of seventy-one.

*Name:* HASTINGS, SARAH
*Alternative spellings:* Haslings
*Location:* London
*Classification:* Thimble maker
*Other classifications:* Dog collar maker
*Date mark registered:* Unknown
*Active:* ca. 1802
*Marital status at registration:* Widow
*In partnership with:* Son
*Address:* 29 Belvedere Place, Borough Road
*Husband's name:* Joseph Hastings (?)
*Source:* Sun Insurance 11936, vol. 423
*Additional information:* Sun Insurance Policy No.
370462, registered April 15, 1802: on
household goods, wearing apparel £125, china
and glass £10, stock and utensils £165. Sun
Insurance Policy No. 730959, registered May 4,
1802: £300 total. Son's name was perhaps
Thomas Hastings (Grimwade, p. 539).

*Name:* HATFIELD, SUSANNAH
*Location:* London
*Classification:* Goldsmith
*Date mark registered:* April 14, 1740
*Marital status at registration:* Widow
*Address:* St. Martin's Lane

*Husband's name:* Charles Hatfield (?)
*Husband's classification:* Largeworker
*Source:* Grimwade, p. 540
*Additional information:* Charles Hatfield was one of the Subordinate Goldsmiths to the King, 1723–39.

*Name:* HAYWARD, ELIZABETH
*Location:* Salisbury
*Classification:* Unknown
*Date mark registered:* Unknown
*Active:* Post-1677–ca. 1699
*Marital status at registration:* Widow
*Husband's name:* Thomas Hayward
*Source:* Kent research
*Additional information:* Thomas Hayward died in 1677. Elizabeth Hayward was fined by the Goldsmiths' Company in London in 1699.

*Name:* HEDLEY, JANE
*Maiden name:* Gamsby
*Location:* Durham
*Classification:* Goldsmith
*Other classifications:* Jeweler
*Date mark registered:* Unknown
*Active:* 1811–22
*Marital status at registration:* Unknown
*Address:* Sadler Street
*Husband's name:* Anthony Hedley
*Husband's classification:* Silversmith
*Source:* Gill, p. 115
*Additional information:* Jane and Anthony Hedley were married August 1, 1789. He was active as a silversmith from 1789 to 1811. Jane Hedley carried on the business after not being able to find a purchaser for the premises.

*Name:* HENSON, MARY
*Location:* London
*Classification:* Clockmaker
*Date mark registered:* Unknown
*Active:* ca. 1726
*Marital status at registration:* Single woman
*In partnership with:* Sarah Henson (sister)
*Address:* Well Yard, Little Britain, parish of St. Bartholomew
*Source:* Sun Insurance 11936, vol. 23, p. 344
*Additional information:* Sun Insurance Policy No. 40684, registered January 23, 1726: on household goods and stock in dwelling house (being their own) £200, goods in trust £300.

*Name:* HENSON, SARAH
*Location:* London
*Classification:* Clockmaker
*Date mark registered:* Unknown

*Active:* ca. 1726
*Marital status at registration:* Single woman
*In partnership with:* Mary Henson (sister)
*Address:* Well Yard, Little Britain, parish of St. Bartholomew
*Source:* Sun Insurance 11936, vol. 23, p. 344
*Additional information:* Sun Insurance Policy No. 40684, registered January 23, 1726: on household goods and stock in dwelling house (being their own) £200, goods in trust £300.

*Name:* HILL, ANN
*Location:* London
*Classification:* Free goldsmith
*Other classifications:* Largeworker
*Date mark registered:* July 15, 1726
*Active:* 1726–ca. 1737
*Marital status at registration:* Widow (?)
*Address:* Great Trinity Lane
*Source:* Grimwade, pp. 545–46
*Additional information:* Ann Hill's first mark was unusual in that it incorporated the year of entry under the initials, as commonly done in Scandinavia. Second mark, undated, registered between May 1734 and December 1735, at Albemarle Street. Ann Hill was perhaps mother of Caleb Hill.

*Name:* HILLARY, MARY
*Location:* Cork
*Classification:* Unknown
*Date mark registered:* 1784
*Marital status at registration:* Unknown
*Address:* 46 North Main Street
*Source:* Bennett (1972), p. 349
*Additional information:* Registered by Dublin Goldsmiths' Company.

*Name:* HILLIER, HANNAH
*Location:* London
*Classification:* Watchmaker
*Date mark registered:* Unknown
*Marital status at registration:* Unknown
*Address:* Peartree Street, Goswell Street
*Source:* Sun Insurance policies
*Additional information:* Sun Insurance Policy No. 581579, registered (no date given): on household goods in dwelling house £50, wearing apparel £50, utensils and stock £50.

*Name:* HOLADAY, SARAH*
*Alternative spellings:* Holladay, Holiday, Susan
*Location:* London
*Classification:* Goldsmith
*Date mark registered:* July 22, 1719 (in two sizes)

*Active:* 1719–ca. 1740
*Marital status at registration:* Widow
*Address:* Golden Cup in Grafton Street in the parish of St. Anne's in Westminster
*Husband's name:* Edward Holaday
*Husband's classification:* Largeworker
*Source:* Grimwade, p. 549
*Additional information:* Second (sterling) mark registered June 15, 1725. Sun Insurance Policy No. 27663, registered February 2, 1722: £1,000 total.

*Name:* HOLMES, MARY ANN
*Location:* London
*Classification:* Smallworker
*Date mark registered:* May 9, 1826 (incuse mark)
*Active:* 1826–ca. 1834
*Marital status at registration:* Unknown
*Address:* 14 Red Cross Square
*Source:* Grimwade, p. 313
*Additional information:* Second mark registered April 17, 1834.

*Name:* HOWARD, MARY
*Location:* London
*Classification:* Unknown
*Date mark registered:* Unknown
*Active:* ca. 1750
*Marital status at registration:* Unknown
*Source:* Pinchbeck, p. 293
*Additional information:* Goldsmiths' Hall Apprentice Register listed her as apprenticed to Jane Hudson in 1750.

*Name:* HOYTE, FRANCES
*Location:* Little Risendon, Gloucester
*Classification:* Largeworker
*Date mark registered:* Undated, probably April 1697 on commencement of Register
*Marital status at registration:* Widow
*Source:* Grimwade, p. 721
*Additional information:* Although Frances Hoyte was described as a "Widd," there appears to be no record of any male goldsmith of this name working earlier in London.

*Name:* HUDDLESTON, MARY
*Location:* London
*Classification:* Unknown
*Date mark registered:* Unknown
*Active:* Apprenticeship—1723–46
*Marital status at registration:* Unknown
*Source:* Smith, p. 68
*Additional information:* Goldsmiths' Hall Apprentice Register, vol. 7, p. 53 (1744). Freed by service October 1, 1760.

*Name:* HUDSON, JANE
*Location:* London
*Classification:* Unknown
*Date mark registered:* Unknown
*Active:* Post-1750
*Marital status at registration:* Unknown
*Source:* Pinchbeck, p. 293
*Additional information:* Goldsmiths' Hall Apprentice Register listed Mary Howard as her apprentice in 1750.

*Name:* HUDSON, REBECCA
*Location:* Huddersfield, York
*Classification:* Silversmith
*Other classifications:* Ironmonger
*Date mark registered:* Unknown
*Active:* ca. 1798
*Marital status at registration:* Unknown
*Address:* Kirkgate
*Source:* Sun Insurance 11937, vol. 22, p. 375
*Additional information:* Sun Insurance Policy No. 674952, registered February 10, 1798: on dwelling house, shop, offices £200, utensils £350, household goods £100.

*Name:* HUNTINGDON, MARY
*Location:* Chester
*Classification:* Unknown
*Date mark registered:* Unknown
*Active:* 1823–ca. 1828
*Marital status at registration:* Unknown
*Address:* 38 Bridge Street Row (?)
*Source:* Reddaway, p. 89
*Additional information:* Found in Pigot & Co.'s *New Commercial Dictionary* (1828).

*Name:* HUSSEY, ELIZABETH
*Alternative spellings:* Mary (?)
*Location:* London
*Classification:* Smallworker
*Other classifications:* Free haberdasher
*Date mark registered:* Undated, between October 1723 and April 1724
*Marital status at registration:* Widow
*Address:* Exchequer Alley
*Husband's name:* Edward Hussey
*Source:* Grimwade, p. 555

*Name:* HUTCHINSON, ANN
*Maiden name:* Ebdon
*Location:* Durham
*Classification:* Unknown
*Date mark registered:* Unknown
*Active:* ca. 1770
*Marital status at registration:* Widow
*Address:* Sadler Street

*Husband's name:* John Hutchinson
*Husband's classification:* Goldsmith
*Source:* Gill, p. 124
*Additional information:* Widowed within a month of being married.

*Name:* HUTTON, SARAH
*Location:* London
*Classification:* Largeworker
*Other classifications:* Goldsmith
*Date mark registered:* June 20, 1740
*Active:* 1740–ca. 1748
*Marital status at registration:* Widow
*Address:* The Hat and Feather, Goswell Street
*Husband's name:* Samuel Hutton
*Source:* Grimwade, p. 556
*Additional information:* Moved to Noble Street as of March 15, 1748.

*Name:* HYDE, MARY ANN (see Reily, Mary Ann)

*Name:* ISSOD, JOYCE
*Location:* London
*Classification:* Largeworker
*Date mark registered:* Undated, prior to 1702
*Marital status at registration:* Widow
*Address:* Fleet Street
*Husband's name:* Thomas Issod
*Source:* Grimwade, p. 557
*Additional information:* Heal records her here in 1697, following Chaffers, who regarded all the early undated entries as of April 1697.

*Name:* JACKSON, ELIZABETH (see Oldfield, Elizabeth)

*Name:* JACKSON, ELIZABETH
*Location:* Dublin
*Classification:* Unknown
*Date mark registered:* 1827
*Marital status at registration:* Unknown
*Address:* 110 Grafton Street
*Source:* Bennett (1972), p. 311

*Name:* JACKSON, MARY
*Location:* London
*Classification:* Casemaker
*Date mark registered:* January 19, 1793
*Marital status at registration:* Unknown
*Address:* 2 Bridgewater Gardens
*Source:* Grimwade, p. 313

*Name:* JACOBS, REBECCA
*Location:* Portsmouth, Hampshire
*Classification:* Silversmith

*Other classifications:* Shopseller
*Date mark registered:* Unknown
*Active:* ca. 1800
*Marital status at registration:* Unknown
*Address:* 4 Bath Square
*Source:* Sun Insurance 11937, vol. 29, p. 640
*Additional information:* Sun Insurance Policy No. 699047, registered February 1, 1800: on household goods, wearing apparel, plate, and books £150, utensils and stock £200, plate £150.

*Name:* JAGO, MAHALA
*Location:* London
*Classification:* Smallworker
*Date mark registered:* September 4, 1830
*Marital status at registration:* Widow
*Address:* 6 Tabernacle Row
*Husband's name:* John or James Jago
*Husband's classification:* Smallworker
*Source:* Grimwade, p. 559
*Additional information:* Culme, p. 256.

*Name:* JAQUES, SARAH
*Location:* London
*Classification:* Free clockmaker
*Date mark registered:* March 21, 1721 (incuse mark)
*Marital status at registration:* Unknown
*In partnership with:* John Lee I
*Address:* Angel Court, Snowhill
*Source:* Grimwade, p. 579
*Additional information:* John Lee I entered a second mark alone in 1725 at the same address.

*Name:* JAQUIN, ANN
*Location:* London
*Classification:* Unknown
*Date mark registered:* Unknown
*Active:* Apprenticeship—1723–46
*Marital status at registration:* Unknown
*Source:* Goldsmiths' Hall Apprentice Register, vol. 6, p. 2
*Additional information:* Elizabeth Bence was apprenticed to Jaquin. In 1723 Jaquin herself was apprenticed and freed by service on July 2, 1746.

*Name:* JOHNSON, MARY
*Location:* London
*Classification:* Largeworker
*Date mark registered:* August 17, 1727
*Marital status at registration:* Widow
*Address:* Noble Street, near Goldsmiths' Hall
*Husband's name:* Glover Johnson
*Husband's classification:* Largeworker, freed by

patrimony from Haberdashers' Company
Source: Grimwade, p. 562

Name: JOHNSON, MARY ANNE
Location: Dublin
Classification: Unknown
Date mark registered: Unknown
Active: ca. 1827
Marital status at registration: Widow
Address: 19 Parliament Street
Husband's name: John F. Johnson
Husband's classification: Watchmaker, jeweler
Source: Bennett (1972), p. 312
Additional information: Later moved to 12 Eden Quay (?).

Name: JONES, ELIZABETH*
Location: London
Classification: Plateworker
Date mark registered: January 15, 1783
Marital status at registration: Widow (?)
Address: 49 Bartholomew Close
Husband's name: Robert Jones (?)
Source: Grimwade, p. 563
Additional information: Elizabeth Jones specialized in salvers and trays.

Name: JONES, ELIZABETH
Location: London
Classification: Silversmith
Other classifications: Pawnbroker
Date mark registered: Unknown
Active: ca. 1786
Marital status at registration: Unknown
In partnership with: Isdaile and Isdwil Jones
Address: 93 High Holborn
Source: Sun Insurance 11936, vol. 337, p. 298
Additional information: Sun Insurance Policy No. 517952, registered April 29, 1786: on dwelling house £200, wearing apparel £200, plate £200, utensils and stock goods (in pledge plate and jewels excepted) £400.

Name: KARR, ELIZABETH
Location: Dublin
Classification: Unknown
Date mark registered: Unknown
Active: 1779-83
Marital status at registration: Widow
Address: 85 Grafton Street
Husband's name: John Karr
Husband's classification: Freeman
Source: Bennett (1972), p. 313

Name: KEEN, JANE
Location: Dublin
Classification: Unknown

Date mark registered: 1802
Active: 1802-ca. 1815
Marital status at registration: Widow
Address: 73 Dame Street
Husband's name: William Keen
Husband's classification: Freeman
Source: Bennett (1972), p. 313

Name: KERSILL, ANN
Alternative spellings: Kineard
Location: London
Classification: Largeworker
Date mark registered: June 16, 1747
Marital status at registration: Widow
Address: Foster Lane
Husband's name: Richard Kersill
Husband's classification: Largeworker
Source: Grimwade, p. 569

Name: KING, SUSANNAH
Location: London
Classification: Unknown
Date mark registered: Unknown
Active: Apprenticeship—1705-34
Marital status at registration: Unknown
Source: Smith, p. 68
Additional information: Goldsmiths' Hall Apprentice Register, vol. 4, p. 104 (1705). Freed by service November 12, 1734.

Name: KIRKUP, JANE
Maiden name: Dawson
Location: Newcastle upon Tyne
Classification: Goldsmith
Other classifications: Administrator
Date mark registered: Unknown
Active: ca. 1757
Marital status at registration: Widow
Address: On the Side
Husband's name: James Kirkup
Source: Gill, p. 134
Additional information: Jane Kirkup continued the retail side of the business, probably leaving the manufacturing side in the hands of her son John.

Name: KNIGHT, ANN
Location: London
Classification: Goldworker
Date mark registered: November 14, 1777
Marital status at registration: Unknown
Address: Noble Street
Source: Grimwade, p. 356

Name: LAITHWAIT, ANN
Location: London

Classification: Watchcase maker
Date mark registered: June 30, 1790
Marital status at registration: Widow
Address: 104 Gray's Inn Lane
Husband's name: John Laithwait
Husband's classification: Watchcase maker
Source: Grimwade, p. 333

Name: LAMBE, JANE
Location: London
Classification: Unknown
Date mark registered: Two marks (sterling and new standard) entered undated between January 1719 and July 1722
Active: ca. 1719–ca. 1732
Marital status at registration: Widow
Address: 3 King's Court, Chandos Street
Husband's name: George Lambe
Husband's classification: Largeworker
Source: Grimwade, p. 574
Additional information: Her son Edward John Lambe was apprenticed to her in 1731.

Name: LANGFORD, MARY
Location: London
Classification: Clockmaker
Date mark registered: Unknown
Active: ca. 1761
Marital status at registration: Unknown
Address: The Dial in New Street, Cloth Fair
Source: Sun Insurance 11936, vol. 137, p. 7
Additional information: Sun Insurance Policy No. 180613, registered February 6, 1761: on wearing apparel £30, household goods, utensils, and stock £200.

Name: LANGLANDS, DOROTHY*
Maiden name: Storey
Location: Newcastle upon Tyne
Classification: Goldsmith
Other classifications: Jeweler
Date mark registered: Unknown
Active: 1804–14
Marital status at registration: Widow (?)
Address: Dean Street
Husband's name: John Langlands II
Source: Gill, pp. 138–39
Additional information: Daughter of Charles Storey of Soho, London.

Name: LANGLANDS, MARGARET
Maiden name: Robinson
Location: Newcastle upon Tyne
Classification: Goldsmith
Other classifications: Jeweler
Date mark registered: Unknown

Active: Pre-1795
Marital status at registration: Widow
In partnership with: John Robertson I
Address: In the Side
Husband's name: John Langlands I
Source: Gill, p. 146
Additional information: Margaret and John Langlands I were married April 22, 1764. She was the mother of John Langlands II, who married Dorothy Storey. Her partnership with John Robertson I lasted until 1795. She died in February 1796.

Name: LAUGHTON, ANN
Location: London
Classification: Smallworker
Date mark registered: December 15, 1701
Marital status at registration: Widow
Address: Goat Alley, Whitecross Street
Husband's name: John Laughton I
Husband's classification: Smallworker
Source: Grimwade, p. 576

Name: LAUGHTON, JANE
Location: London
Classification: Smallworker
Other classifications: Free grocer
Date mark registered: April 1697 on commencement of Register
Marital status at registration: Widow (?)
Address: Bedfordbury, near St. Martin's Lane
Husband's name: Charles Laughton I (?)
Husband's classification: Smallworker (?)
Source: Grimwade, p. 576
Additional information: Charles Laughton I may have been her husband or brother.

Name: LAUGHTON, MARY
Location: London
Classification: Smallworker
Date mark registered: October 31, 1704
Marital status at registration: Widow
Address: Noble Street
Husband's name: John Laughton II
Husband's classification: Largeworker
Source: Grimwade, p. 576

Name: LEE, ELIZABETH
Location: London
Classification: Silversmith
Other classifications: Toywoman
Date mark registered: Unknown
Active: ca. 1787
Marital status at registration: Unknown
Address: 469 The Strand
Source: Sun Insurance 11936, vol. 342

*Additional information:* Sun Insurance Policy No. 532088, registered June 29, 1787: on household goods £100, wearing apparel £100, utensils and stock £200.

*Name:* LIGHT, SUSAN
*Location:* Bristol
*Classification:* Goldsmith
*Date mark registered:* Unknown
*Active:* ca. 1683
*Marital status at registration:* Wife
*In partnership with:* John Light (husband)
*Husband's classification:* Goldsmith
*Source:* Kent research
*Additional information:* In 1683 Susan Light journeyed to London on behalf of her husband John to represent him before the London Wardens on a charge of selling substandard plate.

*Name:* LILLY, ELIZABETH
*Location:* London
*Classification:* Unknown
*Date mark registered:* Unknown
*Active:* Apprenticeship—1746–54
*Marital status at registration:* Unknown
*Source:* Smith, p. 68
*Additional information:* Goldsmiths' Hall Apprentice Register, vol. 7, p. 76 (1746). Freed by service June 12, 1754.

*Name:* LOFTHOUSE, MARY
*Location:* London
*Classification:* Largeworker
*Date mark registered:* March 30, 1731
*Marital status at registration:* Widow (?)
*Address:* Maiden Lane, Wood Street
*Husband's name:* Matthew or Seth Lofthouse (?)
*Source:* Grimwade, p. 584
*Additional information:* Different address from either Matthew or Seth Lofthouse.

*Name:* LOVE, ELIZABETH
*Location:* London
*Classification:* Silversmith
*Date mark registered:* Unknown
*Active:* ca. 1781
*Marital status at registration:* Unknown
*Address:* Aldgate High Street
*Husband's name:* James Love
*Source:* Sun Insurance 11936, vol. 229, p. 332
*Additional information:* Sun Insurance Policy for three houses £600. Undated (1781).

*Name:* LOVERIDGE, SARAH
*Location:* Birmingham

*Classification:* Unknown
*Date mark registered:* Unknown
*Active:* ca. 1846
*Marital status at registration:* Unknown
*Source:* Smith, p. 69

*Name:* LYLE, ANNE
*Location:* Southampton
*Classification:* Unknown
*Date mark registered:* Unknown
*Active:* ca. 1631
*Marital status at registration:* Unknown
*Husband's name:* William Lyle
*Source:* Kent research
*Additional information:* "Clearly active in the family business."

*Name:* MACAIRE, ANN (see Desvignes, Ann)

*Name:* McFARLAN, JESSIE
*Alternative spellings:* Mackfarlan, Mackfarlane, Mackfarlen
*Location:* London
*Classification:* Largeworker
*Other classifications:* Plateworker
*Date mark registered:* October 31, 1739
*Marital status at registration:* Widow
*Address:* New Street, Cloth Fair
*Husband's name:* John Mackfarlan
*Husband's classification:* Largeworker, plateworker
*Source:* Grimwade, p. 587

*Name:* MAHON, ANN
*Location:* Westminster
*Classification:* Watchmaker
*Date mark registered:* Unknown
*Active:* ca. 1804–ca. 1810
*Marital status at registration:* Wife
*In partnership with:* James Mahon (husband)
*Address:* 8 Little Queen Street
*Source:* Sun Insurance policies 1804, 1807, 1810
*Additional information:* The Mahons worked in partnership with Isabella and Thomas Bray; also Catherine and John Wright.

*Name:* MAINWARING, MARY
*Location:* London
*Classification:* Goldworker
*Date mark registered:* April 9, 1836
*Marital status at registration:* Widow
*Address:* Chichester Rents, Chancery Lane
*Husband's name:* John Mainwaring
*Husband's classification:* Goldworker
*Source:* Grimwade, p. 375

*Name:* MAKEMEID, MARY
*Location:* London
*Classification:* Plateworker
*Date mark registered:* October 2, 1773
*Marital status at registration:* Widow
*Address:* 115 Shoe Lane
*Husband's name:* Christopher Makemeid
*Husband's classification:* Plateworker
*Source:* Grimwade, p. 589

*Name:* MALCOMSON, RACHEL
*Location:* Lurgan, County Armagh
*Classification:* Unknown
*Date mark registered:* 1785
*Marital status at registration:* Unknown
*Address:* Corner of Castle Lane and Main Street
*Source:* Bennett (1972), p. 354
*Additional information:* Rachel Malcomson registered in Dublin. Thomas Malcomson, who had the same address and may have been Rachel's son, registered in Dublin in 1800.

*Name:* MANGY, KATHERINE
*Alternative spellings:* Mangie, Mangey
*Location:* Hull
*Classification:* Silversmith
*Date mark registered:* Unknown
*Active:* ca. 1680
*Marital status at registration:* Widow (?)
*Husband's name:* Edward Mangy
*Source:* Bennett, Ann, pp. 149–62

*Name:* MANGY, KATHERINE
*Alternative spellings:* Mangie, Mangey
*Location:* Hull
*Classification:* Silversmith
*Date mark registered:* Unknown
*Active:* ca. 1740
*Marital status at registration:* Unknown
*Address:* Church Lane
*Source:* Sun Insurance 11936, vol. 55, p. 370
*Additional information:* Sun Insurance Policy No. 83577, registered March 4, 1740: on household goods £100, utensils and stock £300. Katherine Mangy was born in 1677. She worked for her mother, Katherine Mangy, until the latter's death. She then continued to run the business with her brother. She died in 1747 (Ann Bennett — unpublished).

*Name:* MANJOY, DOROTHY
*Alternative spellings:* Monjoy, Mountjoy
*Location:* Kilkenny
*Classification:* Unknown

*Date mark registered:* Unknown
*Active:* ca. 1715–31
*Marital status at registration:* Widow
*Husband's name:* Benjamin Manjoy
*Husband's classification:* Goldsmith, freeman
*Source:* Bennett (1972), p. 317
*Additional information:* Dorothy Manjoy registered her mark in Dublin. Benjamin Manjoy died in 1715.

*Name:* MARRAM, ELIZABETH
*Location:* London
*Classification:* Smallworker
*Date mark registered:* April 6, 1717
*Marital status at registration:* Widow
*Address:* Fenchurch Street
*Husband's name:* Stephen Marram
*Husband's classification:* Smallworker
*Source:* Grimwade, p. 591

*Name:* MARRIOTT, ELIZABETH
*Location:* London
*Classification:* Smallworker
*Date mark registered:* Undated, between May 10 and May 15, 1739
*Marital status at registration:* Single woman (?)
*Address:* The Black Lion in Chancery Lane
*Source:* Grimwade, p. 592
*Additional information:* No evidence of possible succession to a deceased husband's business.

*Name:* MARYON, JANE
*Alternative spellings:* Maryan
*Location:* Penryn, Exeter
*Classification:* Smallworker (suggested by her mark)
*Date mark registered:* April 2, 1722
*Active:* 1722–26
*Marital status at registration:* Widow
*Husband's name:* Peter Maryon
*Husband's classification:* Huguenot goldsmith
*Source:* Kent research
*Additional information:* Peter Maryon died in 1710. Jane Maryon died in 1726.

*Name:* MATHEW, MARY
*Alternative spellings:* Matthew (?)
*Location:* London
*Classification:* Largeworker
*Other classifications:* Goldsmith
*Date mark registered:* May 28, 1707
*Active:* ca. 1700–ca. 1709
*Marital status at registration:* Widow (?)
*Address:* George Alley, Lombard Street
*Husband's name:* William Mathew I
*Husband's classification:* Largeworker

*Source:* Grimwade, p. 593; Heal, p. 203
*Additional information:* Heal records a Mary
Matthew, goldsmith, in London from 1700 to
1709.

*Name:* MATHEWS, ELIZABETH
*Location:* London
*Classification:* Plateworker
*Date mark registered:* February 17, 1825
*Marital status at registration:* Unknown
*In partnership with:* Robert Mathews (brother or
son?)
*Address:* 3 Horshoe Court, Ludgate Hill
*Source:* Grimwade, p. 593
*Additional information:* Second mark registered
March 15, 1825.

*Name:* MAURICE, MARGUERITE
*Location:* London
*Classification:* Unknown
*Date mark registered:* Unknown
*Marital status at registration:* Unknown
*In partnership with:* Mary Browne
*Source:* Wenham, p. 63

*Name:* MERFIELD, REBECCA
*Location:* London
*Classification:* Smallworker
*Date mark registered:* January 27, 1823
*Marital status at registration:* Widow (?)
*Address:* 111 Goswell Street
*Husband's name:* Samuel Flight Merefield (?)
*Husband's classification:* Goldsmith
*Source:* Grimwade, p. 594
*Additional information:* Related to James Merfield,
smallworker (?)

*Name:* MILLER, ANN
*Location:* Bristol
*Classification:* Smallworker
*Other classifications:* Bucklemaker
*Date mark registered:* January 16, 1764
*Active:* 1764–ca. 1773
*Marital status at registration:* Widow (?)
*Address:* Broad Street (?)
*Husband's name:* Miller (?)
*Husband's classification:* Jeweler (?)
*Source:* Grimwade, p. 718
*Additional information:* Ann Miller registered her
mark in London. A jeweler by the name of
Miller died in December 1762; this may have
been Ann Miller's husband.

*Name:* MILLS, DOROTHY* (see Sarbitt,
Dorothy)

*Name:* MONK, ANN
*Alternative spellings:* Monck
*Location:* London
*Classification:* Unknown
*Date mark registered:* Unknown
*Active:* Apprenticeship—1756–64
*Marital status at registration:* Unknown
*Source:* Smith, p. 68
*Additional information:* Goldsmiths' Hall
Apprentice Register, vol. 7, p. 231 (1756).
Freed by service December 5, 1764.

*Name:* MOORE, ESTHER
*Alternative spellings:* Moor
*Location:* London
*Classification:* Goldworker
*Date mark registered:* January 12, 1774
*Marital status at registration:* Widow
*Address:* 37 Gracechurch Street
*Husband's name:* Edward Moore
*Husband's classification:* Goldworker, smallworker
*Source:* Grimwade, p. 599

*Name:* MORLEY, ELIZABETH*
*Location:* London
*Classification:* Smallworker
*Other classifications:* Cutler, dealer in toys,
goldsmith, silversmith
*Date mark registered:* August 8, 1794
*Active:* 1794–ca. 1807
*Marital status at registration:* Widow
*Address:* 7 Westmoreland Buildings, Aldersgate
Street
*Husband's name:* Thomas Morley
*Husband's classification:* Plateworker
*Source:* Grimwade, p. 600
*Additional information:* Second mark registered
July 19, 1796; third October 1, 1800. Sun
Insurance Policy, registered April 15, 1797:
£200 total. Sun Insurance Policy, registered
April 15, 1807: £300 total.

*Name:* MUNS, ELIZABETH*
*Location:* London
*Classification:* Smallworker
*Date mark registered:* May 3, 1768
*Marital status at registration:* Widow (?)
*Address:* 3 Bull and Mouth Street, St. Martin's
Le Grand
*Husband's name:* John Muns (?)
*Husband's classification:* Largeworker (?)
*Source:* Grimwade, p. 604
*Additional information:* Elizabeth Muns appears to
have worked for only a year after her husband's
death.

*Name:* NAN, MARGRETT
*Location:* London
*Classification:* Casemaker
*Date mark registered:* No date (incuse mark)
*Marital status at registration:* Widow (?)
*Address:* New Street, near Shoe Lane
*Husband's name:* George Nan (?)
*Husband's classification:* Free clockmaker (?)
*Source:* Grimwade, p. 314

*Name:* NASH, ELIZA
*Alternative spellings:* Elizabeth (?)
*Location:* London
*Classification:* Goldworker
*Date mark registered:* March 27, 1824
*Active:* 1824–ca. 1828
*Marital status at registration:* Unknown
*Address:* 2 Red Lion Square, Clerkenwell
*Source:* Grimwade, p. 359
*Additional information:* Second mark registered
April 28, 1828. Moved to 74 Myddleton Street
as of April 29, 1828.

*Name:* NEED, SUSANNA
*Location:* London
*Classification:* Casemaker
*Date mark registered:* April 13, 1804
*Marital status at registration:* Unknown
*Address:* 27 Rawstone Street, St. John's Street
Road
*Husband's name:* Bartholomew Need
*Source:* Grimwade, p. 318

*Name:* NOLAN, ANN
*Location:* Loughrea, County Galway
*Classification:* Unknown
*Date mark registered:* 1784
*Marital status at registration:* Unknown
*Address:* Main Street
*Source:* Bennett (1972), p. 355
*Additional information:* Ann Nolan registered her
mark in Dublin.

*Name:* NORTHCOTE, HANNAH*
*Maiden name:* Coley
*Location:* London
*Classification:* Goldsmith
*Date mark registered:* June 6, 1798
*Active:* 1798–ca. 1831
*Marital status at registration:* Widow
*Address:* Barkley Street, Clerkenwell
*Husband's name:* Thomas Northcote
*Husband's classification:* Spoonmaker
*Source:* Grimwade, p. 609
*Additional information:* Daughter of Simeon
Coley, bucklemaker. She was born about

1761. Married Thomas Northcote on January
12, 1788. Second mark registered December 3,
1799. Moved to 9 Cross Street, Hatton
Garden, as of March 4, 1800. Hannah
Northcote died September 9, 1831. She was
buried in Bunhill Fields, where there is a
monument to her.

*Name:* NORVILL, JANE
*Location:* London
*Classification:* Watchcase maker
*Date mark registered:* March 8, 1819
*Marital status at registration:* Widow
*Address:* Domingo Street, St. Luke's
*Husband's name:* James Norvill
*Husband's classification:* Watchcase maker
*Source:* Grimwade, p. 343

*Name:* OLDFIELD, ELIZABETH
*Married name (?):* Elizabeth Jackson
*Location:* London
*Classification:* Largeworker
*Other classifications:* Plateworker
*Date mark registered:* August 4, 1748
*Active:* 1748–ca. 1754
*Marital status at registration:* Widow (?)
*Address:* Paternoster Row
*First husband's name:* Charles Jackson (?)
*Husband's classification:* Largeworker (?)
*Source:* Grimwade, pp. 558, 610
*Additional information:* Second mark registered as
Elizabeth Oldfield with no explanation for
change of name December 19, 1750; third
September 5, 1754.

*Name:* OSMENT, ELIZABETH
*Location:* Exeter
*Classification:* Unknown
*Date mark registered:* Unknown
*Active:* ca. 1854
*Marital status at registration:* Widow
*Husband's name:* John Osment
*Source:* Kent research
*Additional information:* Continued the business
after her husband's death in 1854.

*Name:* OWEN, MARY
*Location:* London
*Classification:* Smallworker
*Date mark registered:* January 17, 1739
*Active:* 1739–ca. 1745
*Marital status at registration:* Widow
*Address:* Wheatsheaf, upper end of Cheapside
*Husband's name:* William Owen
*Husband's classification:* Smallworker
*Source:* Grimwade, p. 611

*Additional information:* William Owen was Free of the Fishmongers' Company.

*Name:* PACKER, ELIZABETH
*Location:* Reading
*Classification:* Watchmaker
*Other classifications:* Silversmith
*Date mark registered:* Unknown
*Active:* ca. 1811
*Marital status at registration:* Unknown
*Source:* Sun Insurance 11937, vol. 94
*Additional information:* Sun Insurance Policy No. 855460, registered February 19, 1811: on dwelling house in Minster Street £500, dwelling house, wearing apparel, and plate £100, utensils and stock £200, workshop £50, house in Market Place in private tenure £200.

*Name:* PADMORE, ELIZA
*Alternative spellings:* Elizabeth (?)
*Location:* London
*Classification:* Bucklemaker
*Date mark registered:* August 29, 1774
*Marital status at registration:* Widow
*Address:* 19 Firth Street, Soho
*Husband's name:* George Padmore
*Husband's classification:* Bucklemaker
*Source:* Grimwade, p. 611

*Name:* PAGITTER, MRS.
*Location:* London
*Classification:* Silversmith
*Date mark registered:* Unknown
*Active:* Early 18th century
*Marital status at registration:* Unknown
*Address:* Near St. Duncan's Church, Fleet Street
*Source:* Smith, p. 67
*Additional information:* Retailer who advertised as silversmith in newspaper.

*Name:* PANTIN, MARY
*Alternative spellings:* Pantains, Marie (?)
*Location:* London
*Classification:* Largeworker
*Date mark registered:* August 14, 1733
*Active:* 1733–ca. 1735
*Marital status at registration:* Widow
*Address:* Green Street, Leicester Fields
*Husband's name:* Simon Pantin II
*Husband's classification:* Goldsmith
*Source:* Grimwade, p. 613
*Additional information:* Huguenot (?). See *Huguenot Society Publications*, no. 26, and *Huguenot Society Proceedings*, no. 14, p. 548.

*Name:* PARKER, SUSANNA
*Location:* Greenwich, Kent
*Classification:* Watchmaker
*Other classifications:* Silversmith
*Date mark registered:* Unknown
*Active:* ca. 1777
*Marital status at registration:* Unknown
*Address:* Church Street
*Source:* Sun Insurance 11936, vol. 254, p. 593
*Additional information:* Sun Insurance Policy No. 381518, registered March 21, 1777: on household goods in dwelling house £120, wearing apparel £80, utensils and stock (plate included) £200.

*Name:* PARR, SARAH
*Location:* London
*Classification:* Largeworker
*Date mark registered:* June 20, 1728
*Active:* 1728–ca. 1732
*Marital status at registration:* Widow
*Address:* Cheapside
*Husband's name:* Thomas Parr I
*Husband's classification:* Largeworker
*Source:* Grimwade, p. 615

*Name:* PAYNE, ANN
*Location:* London
*Classification:* Spoonmaker
*Date mark registered:* October 25, 1834
*Marital status at registration:* Widow
*Address:* 21 Great Mitchell Street, St. Luke's
*Husband's name:* James Payne
*Husband's classification:* Spoonmaker
*Source:* Grimwade, p. 616
*Additional information:* Second mark registered November 26, 1834; third December 5, 1834.

*Name:* PEARD, MRS.
*Location:* Barnstaple, Devon
*Classification:* Unknown
*Date mark registered:* Unknown
*Active:* 1680s
*Marital status at registration:* Widow
*Husband's name:* John Peard I
*Source:* Kent research
*Additional information:* Continued the business, using her husband's marks, during the 1680s until her son John Peard II was old enough to take over.

*Name:* PEAREE, ANN
*Alternative spellings:* Perry (?)
*Location:* London
*Classification:* Smallworker
*Date mark registered:* July 13, 1765

*Marital status at registration:* Unknown
*Address:* Old Street Square
*Source:* Grimwade, pp. 18, 617

*Name:* PEPPIN, SUSANNAH
*Location:* London
*Classification:* Smallworker
*Date mark registered:* March 9, 1835
*Marital status at registration:* Widow
*Address:* 20 Kirby Street, Hatton Garden
*Husband's name:* Sydenham William Peppin
*Husband's classification:* Plateworker
*Source:* Grimwade, p. 619

*Name:* PERO, ISABEL
*Maiden name:* Yarnton
*Alternative spellings:* Isabella
*Location:* London
*Classification:* Largeworker
*Date mark registered:* May 1, 1741
*Marital status at registration:* Widow
*Address:* Orange Court, near Leicester Fields
*Husband's name:* John Pero
*Husband's classification:* Largeworker
*Source:* Grimwade, p. 620
*Additional information:* Isabel and John Pero
were married on December 16, 1736. John
Pero possibly a Huguenot. See *Huguenot Society
Proceedings*, no. 13, p. 67.

*Name:* PEYTON, JANE
*Location:* London
*Classification:* Casemaker
*Date mark registered:* December 21, 1797
*Marital status at registration:* Unknown
*Address:* 13 Old Street Square
*Source:* Grimwade, p. 311

*Name:* PHILLIP, PHYLLIS
*Location:* London
*Classification:* Unknown
*Date mark registered:* Unknown
*Active:* ca. 1720
*Marital status at registration:* Unknown
*Source:* Smith, p. 69

*Name:* PIERS, MARY
*Location:* London
*Classification:* Largeworker
*Date mark registered:* June 2, 1758
*Active:* 1758–ca. 1762
*Marital status at registration:* Widow
*Address:* Spur Street, Leicester Fields
*Husband's name:* Daniel Piers
*Husband's classification:* Largeworker
*Source:* Grimwade, p. 624

*Name:* PLATT, MARY
*Location:* Birmingham
*Classification:* Bucklemaker
*Date mark registered:* Unknown
*Active:* ca. 1834
*Marital status at registration:* Unknown
*Source:* Smith, p. 69

*Name:* PRETTY, CATHERINE
*Location:* London
*Classification:* Smallworker
*Date mark registered:* March 13, 1759
*Marital status at registration:* Unknown
*Address:* Gorgs (George's ?) Court, St. John's
Lane, Clerkenwell
*Source:* Grimwade, p. 632
*Additional information:* Moved to Duck Lane,
Smithfield, as of March 21, 1761.

*Name:* PRICE, SAREY
*Location:* London
*Classification:* Smallworker
*Date mark registered:* June 27, 1761
*Marital status at registration:* Unknown
*Address:* Blue Anchor Alley, Bunhill Row
*Source:* Grimwade, p. 633
*Additional information:* Second mark registered
June 14, 1763.

*Name:* PRITCHARD, SARAH
*Location:* London
*Classification:* Knifehaft maker
*Date mark registered:* February 19, 1831
*Marital status at registration:* Widow
*Address:* 28 Steward Street
*Husband's name:* Joseph Pritchard
*Husband's classification:* Platemaker, knifehaft
maker
*Source:* Grimwade, pp. 410, 633
*Additional information:* Signed with an *X*.

*Name:* PURTON, FRANCES
*Location:* London
*Classification:* Smallworker
*Date mark registered:* March 4, 1783
*Active:* 1783–ca. 1795
*Marital status at registration:* Widow
*Address:* 2 Carey Lane
*Husband's name:* Robert Purton
*Husband's classification:* Goldsmith
*Source:* Grimwade, p. 634
*Additional information:* Second mark registered
June 16, 1787; third, in partnership with
Thomas Johnson, February 28, 1793; fourth,
alone, January 28, 1795. Joseph Thredder was
apprenticed to her in 1790.

*Name:* PURVER, SARAH
*Location:* London
*Classification:* Spoonmaker
*Date mark registered:* September 23, 1817
*Marital status at registration:* Widow
*Address:* 2 Clerkenwell Close
*Husband's name:* Thomas Purver
*Husband's classification:* Spoonmaker
*Source:* Grimwade, p. 634

*Name:* RAMSAY, ELIZABETH
*Second married name:* Young
*Location:* Newcastle upon Tyne
*Classification:* Goldsmith
*Date mark registered:* September 15, 1702
*Active:* 1702–ca. 1705
*Marital status at registration:* Widow
*Address:* The Close and the Key
*Husband's name:* John Ramsay
*Source:* Gill, p. 196
*Additional information:* Married former apprentice John Young, probably in 1705.

*Name:* RAMSAY, MARGARET
*Alternative spellings:* Mary
*Location:* Newcastle upon Tyne
*Classification:* Unknown
*Date mark registered:* Unknown
*Active:* ca. 1702
*Marital status at registration:* Widow
*Husband's name:* William Ramsay II
*Source:* Gill, p. 197; Smith, p. 69

*Name:* REASEY, MARY
*Location:* London
*Classification:* Smallworker
*Other classifications:* Watchcase maker
*Date mark registered:* March 2, 1773
*Marital status at registration:* Widow
*Address:* Compton Street, Soho
*Husband's name:* James Reasey
*Husband's classification:* Smallworker
*Source:* Grimwade, p. 638
*Additional information:* Listed in Parliamentary Report of 1773.

*Name:* REILY, HANNAH
*Location:* Kilkenny
*Classification:* Unknown
*Date mark registered:* 1784
*Marital status at registration:* Unknown
*Address:* High Street
*Source:* Bennett (1972), p. 355
*Additional information:* Cork goldsmith registered at Dublin.

*Name:* REILY, MARY ANN
*Alternative spellings:* Riley

*First married name:* Hyde
*Location:* London
*Classification:* Smallworker
*Other classifications:* Working goldsmith
*Date mark registered:* November 28, 1799
*Active:* 1799–ca. 1829
*Marital status at registration:* Widow
*In partnership with:* 1) John Riley; 2) Charles Reily (son?)
*Address:* 6 Carey Lane
*Husband's name:* John Riley/Reily
*Husband's classification:* Smallworker
*Source:* Grimwade, pp. 556, 639
*Additional information:* First mark registered as Mary Hyde, in partnership with John Riley, in 1799. John Riley entered marks alone, under the spelling of Reily, from 1801 to 1826. John Reily was buried May 15, 1826. Second mark as Mary Reily in partnership with Charles Reily, presumably her son, entered May 31, 1826. Charles Reily entered his mark with another partner in January 1829, by which date Mary Ann Reily presumably had retired or died. Sun Insurance Policy No. 700425, registered March 3, 1800: £500 total.

*Name:* REVILL, CHARLOTTE
*Location:* Dublin
*Classification:* Silverplater
*Date mark registered:* Unknown
*Active:* ca. 1813–ca. 1819
*Marital status at registration:* Unknown
*Address:* 17 Sycamore Alley
*Source:* Bennett (1972), p. 326

*Name:* RHODES, MARY
*Alternative spellings:* Rood (?)
*Location:* York
*Classification:* Goldsmith
*Date mark registered:* Unknown
*Active:* ca. 1733
*Marital status at registration:* Widow
*Address:* Collier Gate, Christchurch
*Source:* Sun Insurance 11936, vol. 37, p. 561
*Additional information:* Sun Insurance Policy No. 60635, registered May 3, 1733: on dwelling house £300.

*Name:* RIBLEOU, MARY (?)
*Location:* London
*Classification:* Casemaker (?)
*Date mark registered:* December 30, 1767 (incuse mark)
*Marital status at registration:* Unknown
*Source:* Grimwade, p. 313

Name: RICCARD, CATHERINE
Location: London
Classification: Silversmith
Other classifications: Toywoman
Date mark registered: Unknown
Active: ca. 1787
Marital status at registration: Unknown
Address: Castle Street, Leicester Fields
Source: Sun Insurance 11936, vol. 342
Additional information: Sun Insurance Policy No. 531448, registered June 13, 1787: on dwelling house £800, dwelling house in Brompton Park £350, wearing apparel £50, utensils and stock £3,000.

Name: RICHARDSON, MARY
Location: London
Classification: Smallworker
Other classifications: Bucklemaker
Date mark registered: June 9, 1763
Marital status at registration: Widow
Address: St. John's Square, Clerkenwell
Husband's name: George Richardson
Husband's classification: Plateworker
Source: Grimwade, p. 642
Additional information: Second mark registered October 7, 1763; third November 13, 1765.

Name: RIPSHEAR, MARTHA
Location: London
Classification: Smallworker
Date mark registered: December 1, 1720
Marital status at registration: Widow (?)
Address: Gutter Lane
Husband's name: Thomas Ripshear (?)
Husband's classification: Smallworker, Free Grocer (?)
Source: Grimwade, p. 642

Name: ROBERTS, MARY
Location: Bristol
Classification: Unknown
Date mark registered: Unknown
Active: ca. 1679–ca. 1715
Marital status at registration: Widow
Husband's name: John Roberts
Source: Kent research
Additional information: Continued business after husband's death in 1679. Fined by the London Goldsmiths' Company in 1683, 1699, and 1706 for selling substandard wares. Mary Roberts died in 1715.

Name: ROBERTSON, ANN*
Maiden name: Bryan
Location: Newcastle upon Tyne

Classification: Goldsmith
Other classifications: Jeweler
Date mark registered: 1800
Marital status at registration: Widow (?)
Address: Dean Street
Husband's name: John Robertson I
Husband's classification: Goldsmith and jeweler
Source: Gill, p. 220; Valentine manuscript
Additional information: Ann and John Robertson were married June 4, 1787. Upon John Robertson's death in 1801, Ann was left the household goods, the choice of two cows and an annuity of £100, as well as power of administration over her nephew's inheritance until he came of age.

Name: ROBINS, MARY
Location: London
Classification: Silversmith
Date mark registered: Unknown
Active: ca. 1816
Marital status at registration: Unknown
Address: 13 Fleet Street
Source: Sun Insurance 11936, vol. 466
Additional information: Sun Insurance Policy No 921829, registered August 14, 1816: on dwelling house, wearing apparel, plate, and printed books £200, utensils and stock £350.

Name: ROBINSON, JANE
Maiden name: Thompson
Location: Durham
Classification: Unknown
Date mark registered: Unknown
Active: ca. 1785
Marital status at registration: Single woman
Address: Elvet Bridge
Source: Gill, p. 232
Additional information: Continued father's business after his death in 1785, until her marriage in 1786.

Name: ROKER, ELIZABETH
Location: London
Classification: Plateworker
Date mark registered: October 11, 1776
Marital status at registration: Widow
Address: Bishopsgate Without
Husband's name: Robert Roker III
Husband's classification: Spoonmaker
Source: Grimwade, p. 645

Name: ROMAN, ANN
Location: London
Classification: Largeworker
Date mark registered: Undated, probably April

1697 on commencement of Register
*Marital status at registration:* Single woman (?)
*Address:* Water Lane, Fleet Street
*Source:* Grimwade, p. 646
*Additional information:* Two marks entered.
Grimwade lists no man of this name.

*Name:* ROOD, MARY*
*Maiden name:* Roode
*Location:* London
*Classification:* Largeworker
*Date mark registered:* December 2, 1721 (two
marks, sterling and new standard)
*Marital status at registration:* Widow (?)
*Address:* Maiden Lane
*Husband's name:* James Rood (?)
*Husband's classification:* Largeworker (?)
*Source:* Grimwade, p. 647

*Name:* ROODE, MARY
*Location:* London
*Classification:* Smallworker
*Date mark registered:* October 24, 1738
*Marital status at registration:* Widow
*Address:* Golden Lane
*Husband's name:* Gundry Roode
*Husband's classification:* Largeworker
*Source:* Grimwade, p. 646

*Name:* ROOKE, MARGARET
*Location:* Dublin
*Classification:* Silverplater
*Date mark registered:* Unknown
*Active:* ca. 1819–ca. 1830
*Marital status at registration:* Unknown
*Address:* 15 Lower Exchange Street
*Source:* Bennett (1972), p. 327

*Name:* RUDKIN, MARY
*Location:* Carlow
*Classification:* Unknown
*Date mark registered:* 1784
*Marital status at registration:* Unknown
*Address:* Byrne Street
*Source:* Bennett (1972), p. 355
*Additional information:* Registered at Dublin.

*Name:* RYDER, MARY
*Location:* London
*Classification:* Smallworker
*Date mark registered:* July 4, 1769
*Active:* 1769–ca. 1773
*Marital status at registration:* Unknown
*Address:* Wich Street
*Source:* Grimwade, p. 650

*Name:* SARBITT, DOROTHY*
*Alternative spellings:* Sarbit
*First married name:* Mills
*Location:* London
*Classification:* Largeworker
*Date mark registered:* April 6, 1752
*Active:* ca. 1746–ca. 1754
*Marital status at registration:* Widow
*Address:* Saffron Hill
*Husband's name:* Hugh Mills; Thomas Sarbitt
*Husband's classification:* Largeworker (Mills)
*Source:* Grimwade, pp. 597, 651
*Additional information:* Earlier mark identified
from Heal's record of Dorothy Mills in
partnership with "Thomas Sarbit," goldsmith,
from 1746–47 and found also in 1748–49. First
mark registered, as Dorothy Mills, in 1752;
second, as Dorothy Sarbitt, December 13,
1753. The museum's collection includes a
George II salver by Dorothy Sarbitt dated
1754.

*Name:* SCOTT, ELIZABETH
*Location:* London
*Classification:* Unknown
*Date mark registered:* Unknown
*Active:* Apprenticeship—1747–54
*Marital status at registration:* Unknown
*Source:* Smith, p. 68
*Additional information:* Goldsmiths' Hall
Apprentice Register, vol. 7, p. 89 (1747).
Freed by service November 6, 1754.

*Name:* SCRIVENER, DOR
*Alternative spellings:* Dorah, Dorothy (?)
*Location:* London
*Classification:* Smallworker
*Other classifications:* Free cutler
*Date mark registered:* Undated, very likely April
1697 on commencement of Register
*Marital status at registration:* Widow
*Address:* White Alley, Chancery Lane
*Source:* Grimwade, p. 654
*Additional information:* Related to John Scrivener,
also of the Cutlers' Company (?).

*Name:* SEELEY, MARY
*Location:* London
*Classification:* Unknown
*Date mark registered:* Unknown
*Active:* Apprenticeship—1737–44
*Marital status at registration:* Unknown
*Source:* Smith, p. 68
*Additional information:* Goldsmiths' Hall
Apprentice Register, vol. 6, p. 240 (1737).
Freed by service October 3, 1744.

*Name:* SHAW, MARGARET
*Location:* Dublin
*Classification:* Unknown
*Date mark registered:* 1782
*Marital status at registration:* Widow
*Address:* 7 Essex Bridge
*Husband's name:* Richard Shaw
*Husband's classification:* Sword cutler
*Source:* Bennett (1972), p. 328
*Additional information:* Continued business after husband's death in 1782. Second mark registered, in partnership with Archer Shaw (son?), in 1784.

*Name:* SHEENE, ALICE*
*Location:* London
*Classification:* Largeworker
*Date mark registered:* April 29, 1700
*Active:* 1700–ca. 1715
*Marital status at registration:* Widow
*Address:* Ball Alley, Lombard Street
*Husband's name:* Joseph Sheene
*Husband's classification:* Largeworker
*Source:* Grimwade, p. 656

*Name:* SIBLEY, MARY
*Location:* London
*Classification:* Plateworker
*Date mark registered:* February 23, 1836
*Marital status at registration:* Widow
*In partnership with:* Richard Sibley II
*Address:* 30 Red Lion Street, Clerkenwell
*Husband's name:* Richard Sibley I
*Husband's classification:* Plateworker
*Source:* Grimwade, p. 658
*Additional information:* Richard Sibley II apprenticed to his father. Richard Sibley II entered second mark, alone, March 15, 1837, by which time Mary Sibley had presumably retired or died.

*Name:* SIMCOE, RACHAEL
*Location:* London
*Classification:* Smallworker
*Date mark registered:* February 20, 1724
*Marital status at registration:* Widow (?)
*Address:* Maiden Lane
*Husband's name:* Joseph Simcoe (?)
*Husband's classification:* Smallworker (?)
*Source:* Grimwade, p. 659

*Name:* SINGLETON, SUSANNAH
*Location:* Dublin
*Classification:* Cutler
*Date mark registered:* Unknown
*Active:* ca. 1800–ca. 1802

*Marital status at registration:* Unknown
*Address:* 7 Exchange Street
*Source:* Bennett (1972), p. 329
*Additional information:* A Richard Singleton, cutler, was registered and listed in street directories from 1754 to 1809. He appears at the same address from 1778 to 1784.

*Name:* SKEGGS, SARAH
*Location:* London
*Classification:* Silversmith
*Other classifications:* Watchmaker
*Date mark registered:* Unknown
*Active:* 1782–ca. 1791
*Marital status at registration:* Widow
*Address:* Princess Street in Rotherhill
*Husband's name:* William Skeggs
*Husband's classification:* Watchmaker
*Source:* Sun Insurance policies 1782, 1786, 1791
*Additional information:* William Skeggs registered a Sun Insurance Policy in 1802, possibly a son (?).

*Name:* SLACK, HENRIETTA
*Location:* Dublin
*Classification:* Unknown
*Date mark registered:* Unknown
*Active:* 1774 only
*Marital status at registration:* Widow (?)
*Address:* Fishamble Street (?)
*Husband's name:* Benjamin Slack (?)
*Source:* Bennett (1972), p. 329

*Name:* SMITH, ANN
*Location:* London
*Classification:* Silversmith
*Date mark registered:* Unknown
*Active:* ca. 1781–ca. 1791
*Marital status at registration:* Unknown
*Address:* 170 near King Edward Stairs in Wapping
*Source:* Sun Insurance 11936, vol. 294, p. 116; vol. 339, p. 534; and vol. 375, p. 488

*Name:* SMITH, ANNE
*Location:* London
*Classification:* Smallworker
*Date mark registered:* Undated, probably 1697 on commencement of Register
*Active:* 1692–ca. 1698
*Marital status at registration:* Widow
*Address:* Cock Alley, without Cripplegate
*Source:* Grimwade, p. 661
*Additional information:* Free of Coopers' Company, probably by patrimony.

*Name:* SMITH, ANNE*
*Location:* London
*Classification:* Smallworker
*Date mark registered:* July 26, 1771
*Marital status at registration:* Unknown
*In partnership with:* Nathaniel Appleton
*Address:* Aldersgate Street
*Source:* Grimwade, p. 661
*Additional information:* Partnership appears in Parliamentary Report list 1773. The Smith and Appleton partnership specialized in salt cellars and small cream jugs.

*Name:* SMITH, MARY
*Location:* London
*Classification:* Pendant maker
*Date mark registered:* November 12, 1812 (incuse mark)
*Marital status at registration:* Unknown
*Address:* 32 Red Lion Street
*Husband's name:* George Smith (?)
*Husband's classification:* Pendant maker
*Source:* Grimwade, p. 313

*Name:* SNATT, SARAH
*Location:* London
*Classification:* Smallworker
*Date mark registered:* September 10, 1817
*Marital status at registration:* Widow
*Address:* 4 Fan Street, Aldersgate
*Husband's name:* Josiah Snatt
*Husband's classification:* Smallworker
*Source:* Grimwade, p. 665

*Name:* SPRACKMAN, MISS
*Location:* Bristol
*Classification:* Jeweler
*Date mark registered:* Unknown
*Active:* ca. 1765
*Marital status at registration:* Single woman
*Source:* Jones
*Additional information:* Known from Notice of Marriage.

*Name:* STAFFORD, MARY ANN
*Location:* Dublin
*Classification:* Unknown
*Date mark registered:* 1784
*Active:* 1784–ca. 1815
*Marital status at registration:* Widow
*Address:* 1 Crampton Court
*Husband's name:* William Stafford
*Husband's classification:* Toyseller, watchmaker
*Source:* Bennett (1972), p. 330

*Name:* STAMP, FRANCES
*Location:* London

*Classification:* Plateworker
*Date mark registered:* May 12, 1780
*Marital status at registration:* Widow
*Address:* 86 Cheapside
*Husband's name:* James Stamp
*Husband's classification:* Smallworker, later plateworker
*Source:* Grimwade, p. 669

*Name:* STONE, JANE
*Location:* Dublin
*Classification:* Button manufacturer
*Other classifications:* Seal manufacturer
*Date mark registered:* Unknown
*Active:* ca. 1789
*Marital status at registration:* Unknown
*Address:* 2 Simpsons Court
*Source:* Bennett (1972), p. 330

*Name:* SUMNER, ELIZA*
*Alternative spellings:* Summers, Elizabeth
*Location:* London
*Classification:* Spoonmaker
*Date mark registered:* August 31, 1809
*Active:* 1809–ca. 1814
*Marital status at registration:* Single woman
*In partnership with:* Mary Sumner (mother)
*Address:* 1 Clerkenwell Close
*Source:* Grimwade, p. 674
*Additional information:* Daughter of Mary Sumner. Second mark registered August 21, 1810. Sun Insurance Policy No. 881805, registered May 3, 1813. The museum's collection includes a Regency meat fork by Mary and Eliza Sumner dated 1814.

*Name:* SUMNER, MARY*
*Alternative spellings:* Summers
*Location:* London
*Classification:* Spoonmaker
*Date mark registered:* March 18, 1807
*Active:* 1807–ca. 1814
*Marital status at registration:* Widow
*In partnership with:* Eliza Sumner (daughter)
*Address:* 1 Clerkenwell Close
*Husband's name:* William Sumner I
*Husband's classification:* Plateworker
*Source:* Grimwade, p. 674
*Additional information:* Eliza Sumner was Mary's daughter. Second mark registered in partnership with her daughter August 31, 1809; third mark registered August 21, 1810. The museum's collection includes a Regency meat fork by Mary and Eliza Sumner dated 1814.

*Name:* SWAYNE, FRANCES
*Maiden name:* Burrough
*Alternative spellings:* Swaine
*Location:* Devizes, Wiltshire
*Classification:* Bucklemaker
*Date mark registered:* April 9, 1783 (two marks registered)
*Marital status at registration:* Widow
*Husband's name:* Benjamin Swayne
*Source:* Grimwade, p. 720
*Additional information:* Father was Thomas Burrough.

*Name:* SWEET, MARY
*Location:* Crewkerne, Somerset
*Classification:* Spoonmaker
*Date mark registered:* Unknown
*Active:* 1684–1730
*Marital status at registration:* Widow
*Husband's name:* Edward Sweet
*Source:* Kent research
*Additional information:* Continued the business after her husband's death in 1684.

*Name:* SYNGE, HANNA
*Alternative spellings:* Syng
*Location:* London
*Classification:* Unknown
*Date mark registered:* Unknown
*Active:* Apprenticeship—1681–90
*Marital status at registration:* Unknown
*Source:* Smith, p. 68
*Additional information:* Goldsmiths' Hall Apprentice Register, vol. 3, p. 104 (1681). Freed by service August 19, 1690.

*Name:* TANQUERAY, ANNE*
*Maiden name:* Willaume
*Location:* London
*Classification:* Plateworker
*Date mark registered:* 1724 (two marks, sterling and new standard)
*Active:* 1724–ca. 1733
*Marital status at registration:* Widow (?)
*Address:* Pall Mall
*Husband's name:* David Tanqueray
*Husband's classification:* Largeworker
*Source:* Grimwade, p. 676
*Additional information:* Anne Tanqueray was baptized July 14, 1691. She married David Tanqueray, the apprentice to her father, David Willaume, in 1717. Anne Tanqueray died July 25, 1733. Grimwade reports that Tanqueray is recorded as Subordinate Goldsmith to the King in 1729 and 1732, but it is likely that by this time David Tanqueray

was dead and Anne was running the business on her own.

*Name:* TAYLOR, ELIZABETH
*Location:* London
*Classification:* Smallworker
*Other classifications:* Bucklemaker
*Date mark registered:* February 26, 1767
*Active:* 1767–ca. 1773
*Marital status at registration:* Widow (?)
*Address:* Hugin Alley or Hogan Alley
*Husband's name:* William Taylor
*Husband's classification:* Bucklemaker, smallworker
*Source:* Grimwade, p. 678
*Additional information:* Second mark registered February 26, 1771, as bucklemaker. Appears in Parliamentary Report list of 1773.

*Name:* THEREMIN, FRANCES
*Location:* London
*Classification:* Smallworker
*Date mark registered:* April 24, 1772
*Marital status at registration:* Unknown
*Address:* Spur Street, Leicester Fields
*Source:* Grimwade, p. 680

*Name:* THICKBROOM, JANE
*Location:* London
*Classification:* Watchcase maker
*Date mark registered:* October 30, 1837
*Marital status at registration:* Widow
*Address:* 10 Wellington Street, Clerkenwell
*Husband's name:* George Thickbroom
*Husband's classification:* Watchcase maker
*Source:* Grimwade, p. 344

*Name:* THROPP, ANN
*Location:* Birmingham
*Classification:* Unknown
*Date mark registered:* 1815
*Active:* ca. 1815
*Marital status at registration:* Unknown
*In partnership with:* John Thropp
*Source:* Jackson, p. 366.

*Name:* TIMMINS, JANE
*Location:* Birmingham (?)
*Classification:* Spurmaker
*Date mark registered:* 1818
*Active:* ca. 1818
*Marital status at registration:* Widow (?)
*Source:* Jackson, p. 366

*Name:* TIPPEN, MARIA
*Location:* London

*Classification:* Smallworker
*Date mark registered:* October 10, 1821
*Marital status at registration:* Widow
*Address:* 1 Richmond Buildings, Soho
*Husband's name:* Henry Tippen
*Source:* Grimwade, p. 682

*Name:* TONGE, MARY
*Location:* Dublin
*Classification:* Toyseller
*Other classifications:* Filigree seller
*Date mark registered:* Unknown
*Active:* ca. 1794
*Marital status at registration:* Unknown
*Address:* 44 South Great George's Street
*Source:* Bennett (1972), p. 332

*Name:* TOOKEY, ANNE
*Location:* London
*Classification:* Goldsmith
*Other classifications:* Toywoman, jeweler
*Date mark registered:* Unknown
*Active:* ca. 1791–ca. 1797
*Marital status at registration:* Unknown
*Address:* 45 New Bond Street
*Source:* Sun Insurance 11936, vol. 379, p. 567
and vol. 410
*Additional information:* Sun Insurance Policy,
registered September 17, 1791: on household
goods £300, wearing apparel £200, utensils
and stock £2,000. Sun Insurance Policy No.
670561, registered October 12, 1797: on
household goods £400, wearing apparel £100,
utensils and stock (jewels excepted) £1,000.

*Name:* TOOKEY, ELIZABETH*
*Location:* London
*Classification:* Spoonmaker
*Date mark registered:* Entered in missing register (?)
*Active:* ca. 1768–ca. 1774
*Marital status at registration:* Widow (?)
*Address:* Silver Street
*Husband's name:* James Tookey
*Husband's classification:* Spoonmaker, plateworker
*Source:* Grimwade, p. 683
*Additional information:* Mother of Thomas
Tookey (?). Elizabeth Tookey appears alone in
Parliamentary Report list of 1773.

*Name:* TOWNSEND, FRANCES
*Location:* Dublin
*Classification:* Unknown
*Date mark registered:* Unknown
*Active:* ca. 1788
*Marital status at registration:* Unknown
*Address:* Skinner Row
*Source:* Bennett (1972), p. 332

*Name:* TRENDER, ANN
*Location:* London
*Classification:* Smallworker, goldsmith
*Date mark registered:* November 29, 1792
*Active:* 1792–ca. 1795
*Marital status at registration:* Widow (?)
*In partnership with:* James Trender
*Address:* 10 Princess Street, Barbican
*Husband's name:* Robert Trender (?)
*Husband's classification:* Goldsmith (?)
*Source:* Grimwade, p. 684
*Additional information:* James Trender registered
marks alone as a bucklemaker in April 1793
and August 1797. He entered a mark as a
smallworker, alone, in 1806. Heal records Ann
Trender as a goldsmith in 1795.

*Name:* TRINGHAM, ALICE
*Location:* London
*Classification:* Goldworker
*Date mark registered:* May 30, 1789 (incuse
mark)
*Marital status at registration:* Widow
*Address:* 3 Queens Head Passage
*Husband's name:* John Tringham
*Husband's classification:* Goldworker
*Source:* Grimwade, p. 684

*Name:* TRINGHAM, ANN
*Location:* London
*Classification:* Goldworker
*Date mark registered:* Unknown
*Active:* ca. 1803
*Marital status at registration:* Unknown
*In partnership with:* John and Thomas
Tringham
*Address:* 7 Priest Court, Foster Lane
*Source:* Grimwade, p. 684

*Name:* TROBY, MARY*
*Location:* London
*Classification:* Smallworker
*Date mark registered:* December 17, 1804
*Active:* 1804–ca. 1808
*Marital status at registration:* Widow
*Address:* 2 Ship Court, Old Bailey
*Husband's name:* John Troby
*Source:* Grimwade, p. 685

*Name:* TROWELL, MARY
*Location:* London
*Classification:* Casemaker
*Date mark registered:* March 8, 1766 (incuse
mark)
*Marital status at registration:* Unknown
*Address:* Featherstone Street
*Source:* Grimwade, p. 314

*Name:* TUITE, ELIZABETH
*Location:* London
*Classification:* Largeworker
*Date mark registered:* January 7, 1741
*Active:* 1741–ca. 1769
*Marital status at registration:* Wife (?)
*Address:* George Street, York Buildings
*Husband's name:* John Tuite
*Husband's classification:* Largeworker
*Source:* Grimwade, p. 685
*Additional information:* Grimwade notes the existence of an elegant ewer incorporating both Elizabeth and John Tuite's marks. Heal also records John Tuite, goldsmith, in 1763.

*Name:* TURTON, MEHATABELL
*Location:* London
*Classification:* Smallworker
*Date mark registered:* October 10, 1798
*Marital status at registration:* Widow (?)
*Address:* 31 Monkwell Street
*Husband's name:* William Turton (?)
*Husband's classification:* Smallworker (?)
*Source:* Grimwade, p. 686

*Name:* VEVERS, MARY
*Location:* Hempstead, Hertford
*Classification:* Clockmaker
*Other classifications:* Watchmaker
*Date mark registered:* Unknown
*Active:* ca. 1800
*Marital status at registration:* Unknown
*Source:* Sun Insurance 11937, vol. 30, p. 553
*Additional information:* Sun Insurance Policy No. 698796, registered January 30, 1800: on dwelling house £100, household goods £35, utensils and stock £35, wash house and loft £15, stable and loft £15.

*Name:* WALL, MARY
*Location:* London
*Classification:* Bucklemaker
*Date mark registered:* March 5, 1792 (incuse mark)
*Marital status at registration:* Unknown
*Address:* 6 King's Head Court, St. Martin's Le Grand
*Source:* Grimwade, p. 314

*Name:* WATKINSON, HANNAH
*Location:* Sheffield
*Classification:* Unknown
*Date mark registered:* Unknown
*Active:* ca. 1792
*Marital status at registration:* Unknown
*Source:* Smith, p. 69

*Name:* WHEELER, MARY
*Location:* London
*Classification:* London agent for well-known Birmingham firm of Ledsham, Vale & Wheeler
*Other classifications:* Jeweler
*Date mark registered:* Unknown
*Active:* 1818–56
*Marital status at registration:* Unknown
*In partnership with:* Gervase Wheeler
*Address:* Bartlette's Buildings, Holborn
*Source:* Culme, p. 478

*Name:* WHITFORD, MARY
*Location:* London
*Classification:* Bucklemaker
*Date mark registered:* November 6, 1778
*Marital status at registration:* Unknown
*Address:* 6 St. Martin's Le Grand
*Source:* Grimwade, p. 398
*Additional information:* Second mark, in partnership with William Ballantine, registered January 12, 1779.

*Name:* WILLIAMS, ELIZABETH
*Location:* London
*Classification:* Unknown
*Date mark registered:* Unknown
*Active:* Apprenticeship—1703–12
*Marital status at registration:* Unknown
*Source:* Smith, p. 68
*Additional information:* Goldsmiths' Hall Apprentice Register, vol. 4, p. 93 (1703). Freed by service May 21, 1712.

*Name:* WILLIAMS, JANE
*Location:* London
*Classification:* Bucklemaker
*Date mark registered:* March 6, 1789
*Marital status at registration:* Unknown
*In partnership with:* Elizabeth Barrows
*Address:* 8 Bedford Street, The Strand
*Source:* Grimwade, p. 389

*Name:* WILLIAMS, JANE*
*Maiden name:* Terry
*Location:* Cork
*Classification:* Unknown
*Date mark registered:* 1806
*Active:* 1807–21
*Marital status at registration:* Widow
*In partnership with:* Carden Terry
*Husband's name:* John Williams
*Source:* Smith, p. 69; Bennett (1972), pp. 186–87
*Additional information:* Carden Terry took his

daughter Jane Williams, who registered her mark in Dublin in 1806, into partnership in 1807. She and John Williams were married August 7, 1791. John Williams became Terry's partner in 1795 and died June 13, 1806, leaving five sons and two daughters. Jane Williams died April 17, 1845.

*Name:* WILLIS, MARY
*Location:* London
*Classification:* Bucklemaker
*Date mark registered:* June 27, 1798
*Marital status at registration:* Unknown
*Address:* 81 Bishopsgate Street
*Source:* Grimwade, p. 398

*Name:* WILSON, MARY
*Location:* London
*Classification:* Goldworker
*Other classifications:* Silverworker
*Date mark registered:* Unknown
*Active:* ca. 1771
*Marital status at registration:* Unknown
*Address:* 7 Bells Buildings in Salisbury Court in Fleet Street
*Source:* Sun Insurance 11936, vol. 204, p. 147
*Additional information:* Sun Insurance Policy No. 294477, registered February 14, 1771: on household goods in dwelling house of a bookbinder £50, wearing apparel £50, utensils and stock in trust (plate included) £100.

*Name:* WIMANS, MRS.
*Location:* London
*Classification:* Unknown
*Date mark registered:* Undated, probably April 1697 on commencement of Register
*Marital status at registration:* Widow
*Address:* Foster Lane
*Husband's name:* Edward Wimans
*Husband's classification:* Largeworker
*Source:* Grimwade, p. 706
*Additional information:* Mrs. Wimans struck her mark under her husband's mark, itself undated.

*Name:* WINNE, GRACE
*Location:* London
*Classification:* Smallworker
*Date mark registered:* February 13, 1702
*Marital status at registration:* Unknown
*Address:* Wood Street
*Source:* Grimwade, p. 707

*Name:* WINTER, SARAH
*Location:* London

*Classification:* Goldworker
*Date mark registered:* March 20, 1779
*Marital status at registration:* Unknown
*Address:* 21 Bunhill Road
*Source:* Grimwade, p. 380

*Name:* WITTY, ANN
*Location:* London
*Classification:* Unknown
*Date mark registered:* Unknown
*Active:* Apprenticeship—1702–10
*Marital status at registration:* Unknown
*Source:* Smith, p. 69
*Additional information:* Goldsmiths' Hall Apprentice Register, vol. 4, p. 87 (1702). Freed by service December 6, 1710.

*Name:* WRIGHT, CATHERINE
*Location:* Westminster
*Classification:* Watchmaker
*Date mark registered:* Unknown
*Active:* ca. 1804–ca. 1810
*Marital status at registration:* Wife
*In partnership with:* John Wright (husband)
*Address:* 8 Little Queen Street
*Source:* Sun Insurance policies 1804, 1807, 1810
*Additional information:* The Wrights worked in partnership with Isabella and Thomas Bray; also Ann and James Mahon.

*Name:* WRIGHT, SARAH
*Location:* Southwark
*Classification:* Watchmaker
*Date mark registered:* Unknown
*Active:* ca. 1786
*Marital status at registration:* Wife or widow (?)
*Address:* Long Lane
*Husband's name:* William Wright (?)
*Source:* Sun Insurance 11936, vol. 340, p. 309
*Additional information:* Sun Insurance Policy No. 525002, registered November 29, 1786: on household goods in dwelling house £100, wearing apparel £100, utensils and stock £100.

*Name:* WYNN, MARY
*Location:* London
*Classification:* Goldsmith
*Other classifications:* Pewterer
*Date mark registered:* Unknown
*Active:* Post-1771
*Marital status at registration:* Widow (?)
*Address:* The Golden Dish, Execution Dock, Wapping

*Husband's name:* John Wynn (?)
*Husband's classification:* Goldsmith, pewterer
*Source:* Sun Insurance 11936, vol. 293; p. 368
*Additional information:* Sun Insurance Policy No.
445051, registered on July 2, 1781: on dwelling
house and shop adjoining £200.


*Name:* YELVERTON, LYDIA
*Location:* London
*Classification:* Silversmith

*Other classifications:* Toywoman
*Date mark registered:* Unknown
*Active:* ca. 1791
*Marital status at registration:* Unknown
*Address:* 115 Portland Street
*Source:* Sun Insurance 11936, vol. 382, p. 358
*Additional information:* Sun Insurance Policy No.
594407, registered December 30, 1791: on
household goods in dwelling house £70,
wearing apparel £30, utensils and stock £500.


## Source Citations

BARRETT, Geoffrey N. *Norwich Silver and Its
Marks, 1565–1702.* Norwich: Wensum Press,
1981.

BENNETT, Ann. "The Mangey Family,
Goldsmiths of Hull," *Yorkshire Archaeological
Journal,* vol. 57 (1985).

BENNETT, Douglas. *Irish Georgian Silver.*
London: Cassell, 1972.
———. *Collecting Irish Silver, 1637–1900.*
London: Souvenir Press, 1984.

CULME, John. *The Directory of Gold and
Silversmiths, Jewellers and Allied Traders, 1838–
1914.* Woodbridge, Suffolk: Antique
Collectors' Club, 1987.

GILL, Margaret A. V. *A Directory of Newcastle
Goldsmiths.* London: Worshipful Company of
Goldsmiths, 1980.

GRIMWADE, Arthur. *London Goldsmiths, 1697–
1837: Their Marks and Lives.* 1976. Reprint.
London: Faber, 1982. Several entries based on
the third edition in preparation.

HEAL, Ambrose. *The London Goldsmiths 1200–
1800.* 1935. Reprint. Newton Abbot, Devon:
David & Charles, 1972.

JACKSON, Charles James. *English Goldsmiths
and Their Marks.* 1905. 3rd ed., rev. and enl.
*Silver & Gold Marks of England, Scotland &
Ireland.* Woodbridge, Suffolk: Antique
Collectors' Club, 1989.

JONES, Kenneth Crisp. *The Silversmiths of
Birmingham and Their Marks, 1750–1980.*
London: N.A.G. Press, 1981.

KENT NOTES for Jackson: Refers to
background research pertinent to Timothy
Kent's contribution to Charles James Jackson,
*Silver & Gold Marks of England, Scotland &
Ireland.* Woodbridge, Suffolk: Antique
Collectors' Club, 1989.

KENT RESEARCH: Citation refers to current
research by Timothy Kent on Wessex
silversmiths.

PINCHBECK, Ivy. *Women Workers and the
Industrial Revolution, 1750–1850.* London: G.
Routledge; New York: F. S. Crofts, 1930.

PRIDEAUX, Walter Sherburne. *Memorials of
The Goldsmiths' Company, Being Gleanings from
Their Records between the Years 1335 and 1815.* 2
vols. London: Printed for private circulation by
Eyre and Spottiswoode, 1896–97.

REDDAWAY, Thomas Fiddian, and Lorna E.
M. WALKER. *The Early History of The
Goldsmiths' Company, 1327–1509.* London:
Arnold, 1975.

SMITH, Eric J. G. "Women Silversmiths—
Part I," *The Antique Dealer and Collectors'
Guide,* vol. 23, no. 10 (May 1969): 67–71, 81.

VALENTINE MANUSCRIPT: A list of 141
women silversmiths and 19 apprentices
compiled by Nancy Valentine.

WENHAM, Edward. "Women Recorded as
Silversmiths," *The Antique Collector,* vol. 17
(March/April 1946).

# Collection Checklist

Unless otherwise indicated, all silver in the collection was donated by Mr. and Mrs. Oliver R. Grace, their family, and friends.

Dimensions are given by height, width, and depth.

All hallmark reconstructions, reproduced on the right, were generously provided by Elaine R. S. Hodges, a scientific illustrator at the Smithsonian Institution.

Susanna Barker, London
Three George III wine labels, 1792. Each $\frac{7}{8} \times 1\frac{7}{8}$ in. with 5-in. chain.

Ann Bateman (and Peter Bateman), London
George III tablespoon, 1795. Length: $8\frac{3}{4}$ in.
George III soup ladle, 1796. $13 \times 3\frac{1}{2}$ in.
George III goblet, 1797. $6 \times 3 \times 3$ in.
George III tea caddy spoon, 1797. $3 \times 1\frac{3}{8}$ in.
George III sauce ladle, 1797. $7 \times 2\frac{1}{8}$ in.
George III creamer, 1804. $5\frac{1}{2} \times 5\frac{1}{2} \times 3\frac{1}{4}$ in.

Ann Bateman (with Peter Bateman and William Bateman), London
George III tea set, 1800. Teapot: $7 \times 12 \times 4\frac{1}{2}$ in.; creamer: $4 \times 4\frac{3}{4} \times 2\frac{1}{4}$ in.; sugar bowl: $4\frac{3}{4} \times 6\frac{3}{4} \times 3\frac{3}{4}$ in.
George III plain sugar tongs, 1804. $5\frac{5}{8} \times 1\frac{7}{8} \times \frac{1}{2}$ in.

Hester Bateman, London
George III glass-lined sugar basket, 1777. $5\frac{1}{4} \times 4\frac{1}{4} \times 4\frac{1}{4}$ in.
George III glass-lined mustard pot with spoon, 1778. Pot: $3\frac{1}{4} \times 4 \times 2\frac{1}{4}$ in.; spoon length: $4\frac{1}{4}$ in.
George III circular salver, 1779. $1\frac{1}{2} \times 12\frac{7}{8} \times 12\frac{7}{8}$ in.
George III sugar basket, 1786. $7\frac{1}{2} \times 7\frac{3}{8} \times 4\frac{1}{8}$ in.
George III cake basket, 1788. $6 \times 16\frac{1}{4} \times 11\frac{7}{8}$ in.
George III teapot on stand, 1788. Teapot: $6\frac{3}{4} \times 10\frac{1}{4} \times 3\frac{1}{2}$ in.; stand: $\frac{1}{2} \times 7\frac{1}{8} \times 5$ in.
George III double beaker, 1790. $6 \times 3$ in. (Gift of Mrs. Colin Brown)
George III bright-cut sugar tongs, late 18th/early 19th century. $5\frac{3}{8} \times 1\frac{3}{8} \times \frac{1}{2}$ in.
George III cast sugar tongs, late 18th/early 19th century. $5\frac{3}{8} \times 1\frac{1}{4} \times \frac{5}{8}$ in.

Attributed to Hester Bateman, London
George III coffee pot, 1780. $12\frac{1}{4} \times 9\frac{1}{4} \times 4\frac{5}{8}$ in.

MARGARET BINLEY, London
George III Hermitage wine label, *ca.* 1775.
$1\frac{3}{8} \times 2$ in. with a 3-in. chain.

SARAH BLAKE (and John William Blake),
    London
Six Regency teaspoons, 1812. Length of each:
    $5\frac{1}{2}$ in.
George IV dessert spoon, 1820. Length: $7\frac{1}{4}$ in.
George IV sauce ladle, 1821. Length: $6\frac{7}{8}$ in.

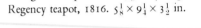

ALICE BURROWS (and George Burrows II),
    London
George III snuff box, 1802. $\frac{3}{4} \times 3\frac{1}{8} \times 2\frac{1}{8}$ in.
George III teapot, 1803. $5\frac{1}{8} \times 9\frac{1}{4} \times 3\frac{1}{2}$ in.
Regency teapot, 1816. $5\frac{1}{8} \times 9\frac{1}{4} \times 3\frac{1}{2}$ in.

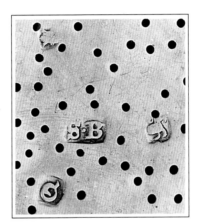

SARAH BUTTALL, London
George III lemon strainer, 1771. $\frac{7}{8} \times 5\frac{3}{4} \times 4\frac{1}{8}$ in.

Attributed to SARAH BUTTALL, London
George III dish cross, 1771. $3 \times 10\frac{3}{4} \times 10\frac{3}{4}$ in.

MARY CHAWNER, London
Six William IV tablespoons, 1835. Length of
    each: $8\frac{3}{4}$ in.
William IV fish slice, 1835. $12\frac{1}{4} \times 2\frac{5}{8}$ in.
Victorian fish slice, 1839. $12\frac{7}{8} \times 3$ in.
Two Victorian dinner forks, 1839. Length of
    each: $8\frac{1}{4}$ in.

ELIZABETH COOKE, London
George III salver, 1767. $1 \times 6\frac{3}{4} \times 6\frac{3}{4}$ in.

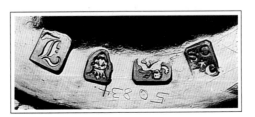

LOUISA COURTAULD (and Samuel Courtauld
    I), London
Pair of George III tea caddies, 1766. Each
    $7\frac{3}{8} \times 4\frac{1}{8} \times 4$ in.

LOUISA COURTAULD (and George Cowles),
   London
George III salver, *ca.* 1777. $\frac{7}{8} \times 6\frac{3}{8} \times 6\frac{3}{8}$ in.

ANN CRAIG (and John Neville), London
George II saucepan, 1742. $4 \times 10\frac{1}{2} \times 5\frac{1}{4}$ in.

Attributed to MARY ANN CROSWELL,
   London
George III child's rattle, 1808. Silver and
   coral. Length: $5\frac{3}{8}$ in.

ELIZABETH EATON, London
Victorian salt spoon, 1849. Length: $4\frac{1}{4}$ in.
Victorian asparagus tongs, 1852. $9\frac{7}{8} \times 2\frac{1}{8}$
   $\times 1\frac{1}{4}$ in.

REBECCA EMES (and William Emes, and
   Edward Barnard), London
George III egg coddler on lamp stand, 1808.
   Coddler: $9\frac{1}{4} \times 6\frac{1}{2} \times 5\frac{3}{8}$ in.; lamp stand:
   $3\frac{3}{8} \times 4\frac{3}{8} \times 3\frac{1}{2}$ in.

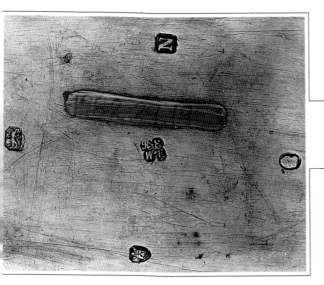

REBECCA EMES (and Edward Barnard),
   London
Four George III sauce tureens with covers,
   1809. Each $5\frac{7}{8} \times 8\frac{1}{4} \times 4\frac{3}{4}$ in.
Regency argyll, 1811. $4\frac{3}{4} \times 7 \times 3\frac{1}{2}$ in.
Regency goblet, 1812. $5 \times 3\frac{1}{2} \times 3\frac{1}{2}$ in.
Regency parcel-gilt mug, 1814. $4\frac{3}{8} \times 5\frac{1}{2} \times 3\frac{1}{8}$ in.
Regency toast rack, 1817. $4\frac{1}{2} \times 6\frac{1}{4} \times 4$ in.
Pair of George IV wine coasters, 1823. Each
   $1\frac{5}{8} \times 6 \times 6$ in.

George IV silver-mounted, two-handled
coconut cup, 1825. $4\frac{3}{8} \times 7 \times 4\frac{3}{8}$ in.
George IV cake basket, 1827. $3\frac{3}{4} \times 11\frac{1}{4} \times 11\frac{1}{4}$ in.

MAGDALEN FELINE, London
George II lamp stand, 1753. $3\frac{3}{4} \times 5\frac{1}{2} \times 5\frac{1}{2}$ in.
George II kettle on lamp stand, 1756.
$9\frac{1}{2} \times 7\frac{1}{4} \times 5\frac{1}{4}$ in.

DINAH GAMON, London
George II creamer, 1743. $3\frac{1}{8} \times 2\frac{7}{8} \times 2\frac{3}{8}$ in.

ELIZABETH GODFREY, London
George II coffee pot, 1743. $6\frac{7}{8} \times 6\frac{3}{4} \times 3\frac{1}{8}$ in.
Pair of George II sauce boats, 1750. Each
$6 \times 8\frac{3}{8} \times 4\frac{1}{2}$ in. (Gift of Faith Corcoran)
Pair of George II tea caddies, 1755.
$5\frac{3}{4} \times 4\frac{3}{8} \times 3\frac{3}{8}$ in.; $5\frac{1}{2} \times 4\frac{1}{4} \times 2\frac{7}{8}$ in.
George II tea caddy, 1758. $5\frac{3}{8} \times 3\frac{1}{2} \times 2\frac{1}{4}$ in.

MARY GOULD, London
Pair of George II silver-gilt candlesticks, 1747.
Each $8 \times 4\frac{3}{8} \times 4\frac{3}{8}$ in.
Note: she used her husband's mark, *IG*.

ELIZABETH HASELWOOD, Norwich
William III oval tobacco box, *ca.* 1695.
$\frac{7}{8} \times 3\frac{3}{4} \times 3$ in.

SARAH HOLADAY, London
George I two-handled cup, 1719. $5\frac{3}{4} \times 8\frac{3}{8} \times 5$ in.
Note: Britannia standard, marked with first two letters of surname.

ELIZABETH JONES, London
George III teapot stand, 1783. $\frac{7}{8} \times 6\frac{1}{4} \times 5$ in.
George III tray, 1795. $1\frac{7}{8} \times 22\frac{3}{8} \times 14\frac{1}{2}$ in.

DOROTHY LANGLANDS, Newcastle upon Tyne
George III tea set, 1809–12. Teapot: $6\frac{1}{2} \times 11 \times 6\frac{1}{4}$ in.; sugar bowl: $4\frac{1}{4} \times 7 \times 4\frac{1}{8}$ in.; creamer: (probably Urquhart and Hart) $3\frac{1}{2} \times 5\frac{3}{8} \times 2\frac{3}{4}$ in.

DOROTHY MILLS (and Thomas Sarbitt), London
See also Dorothy Sarbitt
George II sauce boat, 1748. $4\frac{3}{4} \times 5\frac{1}{4} \times 3\frac{7}{8}$ in.

ELIZABETH MORLEY, London
George III tea caddy spoon, 1797. $2\frac{1}{2} \times 1\frac{3}{8}$ in.
George III tea caddy spoon, 1798. $3\frac{3}{8} \times 1\frac{3}{8}$ in.
George III toddy ladle, 1802. $7 \times 1\frac{7}{8}$ in.

Attributed to ELIZABETH MUNS, London
George III sauce boat, 1768. $4\frac{5}{8} \times 7\frac{3}{8} \times 3\frac{3}{4}$ in.

HANNAH NORTHCOTE, London
George III teapot stand, 1809. $\frac{3}{4} \times 6\frac{3}{8} \times 5$ in.

ANN ROBERTSON, Newcastle upon Tyne
George III fish slice, ca. 1801. Silver with ivory handle. $10\frac{3}{4} \times 3\frac{1}{8}$ in.
George III tea caddy, 1802. $6 \times 5\frac{1}{2} \times 4\frac{3}{8}$ in.
George III creamer and sugar bowl, ca. 1810. Creamer: $4\frac{3}{8} \times 6 \times 2\frac{7}{8}$ in.; sugar bowl: $4\frac{7}{8} \times 8\frac{1}{2} \times 4\frac{1}{8}$ in.

MARY ROOD, London
Pair of George I trencher salts, 1723. Each $1 \times 2\frac{7}{8} \times 2\frac{1}{4}$ in.

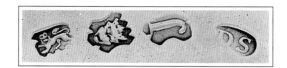

DOROTHY SARBITT, London
See also Dorothy Mills
Pair of George II salvers, 1753. Each
$1 \times 7\frac{1}{2} \times 7\frac{1}{2}$ in.
George II salver, 1754. $1\frac{1}{2} \times 11\frac{3}{8} \times 11\frac{3}{8}$ in.

ALICE SHEENE, London
Queen Anne tankard with cover, 1706.
$7\frac{1}{4} \times 7\frac{5}{8} \times 5\frac{3}{8}$ in.
Note: Britannia standard, marked with first
two letters of surname.

ANNE SMITH (and Nathaniel Appleton),
London
George III cream jug, 1773. $4 \times 4 \times 2\frac{1}{8}$ in.
Set of four George III salt cellars, 1782. Each
$1\frac{1}{2} \times 3 \times 3$ in.

MARY AND ELIZA SUMNER, London
Regency meat skewer, 1811. Length: $11\frac{1}{8}$ in.
Regency marrow scoop, 1812. Length: $9\frac{1}{8}$ in.
Regency meat fork, 1814. Length: $8\frac{1}{4}$ in.

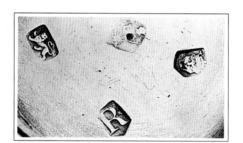

ANNE TANQUERAY, London
Pair of George II silver-gilt salt cellars, 1732.
Each $2\frac{1}{8} \times 3\frac{1}{2} \times 3\frac{1}{2}$ in.

Attributed to ELIZABETH TOOKEY, London
Set of four George II dessert spoons, 1740.
Length of each: $8\frac{1}{4}$ in.
Pair of George II tablespoons, 1740. Length of
each: $8\frac{3}{4}$ in.
George III tablespoon, 1771. Length: $7\frac{7}{8}$ in.

MARY TROBY, London
George III centerpiece, 1808. Silver stand and
glass bowl. Stand: $8 \times 11\frac{1}{4} \times 7\frac{3}{4}$ in.; bowl:
$5 \times 12\frac{1}{4} \times 8\frac{1}{2}$ in.

JANE WILLIAMS (and Carden Terry), Cork
George III marrow scoop, ca. 1810. Length:
$8\frac{1}{4}$ in.
Regency Irish Freedom Box, 1814. $\frac{7}{8} \times 3\frac{7}{8} \times 2\frac{1}{4}$
in. (Gift of Carol and Denis Kelleher)

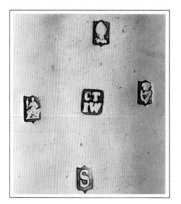 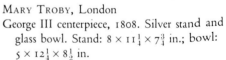

# Glossary

AJOURÉ – the decorative technique of piercing or cutting out shaped holes.

ALLOY – a mixture of metals. Silver, like gold, is too soft to be useful in its pure state, but its ductility, strength, and other positive characteristics are enhanced by the addition of small amounts of copper and other metals. The most common alloys are: sterling (92.5% pure silver, or 11 oz. 2 dwt. to the troy pound of 12 ounces); Britannia standard (95% pure silver); American coin standard (before 1837: 89.2% pure silver; after 1837: 90% pure silver); and an 80% pure silver standard used in much of Europe.

APPRENTICE – a young person, usually between the ages of twelve and twenty-one, bound by indenture to a master silversmith to be trained in the craft. The term of apprenticeship for silver-smithing was generally seven years.

ASSAY – the testing of metal to determine its alloy content. The old cupellation method required the removal of a tiny shaving of silver from the piece to be tested. Modern x-ray fluorescent spectroscopy testing does no damage to the object.

BEADING – in silver, the name of a type of milled or molded edging that looks like a row of tiny beads. Bands of beading often were applied to edges, especially during the neoclassical period.

BRIGHT-CUT ENGRAVING – a form of engraving popular during the neoclassical period by which shallow, irregular chips were removed from the silver surface to achieve a scintillating decorative effect.

CARTOUCHE – a decorative design in the shape of a scroll, a shield, or another form within which a silversmith may engrave a coat of arms or ornamental monogram.

CASTING – to shape in a mold while in liquid form; a piece or part of a piece that has been made by this method. In silver most spouts, finials, feet, and many handles are created by casting.

CAVETTO – the curved or sloped area of a plate, salver, or tray between the flat rim and the horizontal bottom.

CHASING – a decorative technique whereby variously shaped tools are used to compress the silver surface to create patterns without removing any silver. The general outline of the design usually may be discerned on the reverse of a flat surface which has been chased. Chasing is also used to finish parts cast in a mold and to refine repoussé ornamentation.

DIE STAMPING – a method of impressing a design on silver by forcibly pressing it against a carved surface. Small dies or swage blocks were used at the beginning of the 19th century to decorate the backs of spoon bowls or the tips of spoon handles with sculptured designs. Later in the century more complex dies were used for making far more elaborate flatware handles. Bands of die-stamped flowers, fruit, or leaves were set into some hollow ware.

DWT. – the abbreviation for pennyweight, part of the troy weight measurement system equivalent to 1.555 grams.

ELECTROPLATING – a process of depositing pure silver onto a finished base metal object by means of an electric current. This process, which is still in use, was developed in England in the early 1840s and was brought to America shortly thereafter. It was used commercially by 1845. The silver deposited may be very thin or more substantial and durable, depending on the strength of the electrical current and the length of time the object is submerged in an electrolytic bath. Although there was no proper regulation of the industry in the 19th century, various manufacturers designated the levels of quality they produced by such terms as "double," "triple," or "quadruple" plate. Be-cause of the lack of standardization, however, what was called double plate by one firm might be the equivalent of quadruple plate from another. Electroplated wares made "silver" type objects available to the middle class, and even to the working class, by the 1860s and 1870s.

EMBOSSING – another word for repoussé.

ENGRAVING – a decorative technique in which a small amount of silver is scratched or gouged from the surface of an object with a sharp tool called a burin or graver. This technique is particularly suitable for putting initials, names, crests, arms, and special inscriptions on silver. In contrast to chasing, no evidence of the engraving is discernible on the reverse side of a piece.

FLATTING MILL – a machine that uses rollers and pressure to create sheets of silver of uniform thickness from ingots.

FLUTING – concave decoration, usually vertical in direction, like the grooves on the shaft of a classical column. Fluting is the opposite of reeding or ribbing.

GADROONING — a decorative device of alternate convex and concave elements sometimes resembling a ruffle, melon lobes, or a rope-like design. Often used in borders.

INCUSE MARK — a maker's initials stamped into silver with no surrounding shield, diamond, rectangle, or other impression. May indicate that the silversmith was of foreign or provincial origin, or may have another significance as yet undetermined.

JOURNEYMAN — a trained artisan who does not operate a shop but is employed by a master craftsperson. The term, which is derived from the French word for day, indicates that the person is paid by the day rather than by the piece.

LACEBACK SPOON — a type of spoon that has on the back of the bowl relief decoration, often in needlework-like patterns or vine-leaf motifs.

MASTER — a fully trained craftsperson in charge of a shop and authorized to employ journeymen and accept apprentices for training.

MILLED BAND — a strip of silver pressed between rollers, one of which has been carved with a repeat vine, chain, or other design. The resulting band, which has a design on one side, is then used as edging, for plinths, or is set into silver. Milled bands were mass-produced and the same designs may appear on work marked by several different artisans within one geographic area.

MOLDING — a band with a raised and/or indented profile, often used at the edges of seams on a piece of silver and derived stylistically from architectural or wood moldings; something which has been cast in a mold.

PEARLING — an edging of rather large, bead-like protrusions punched out from the reverse of a piece of silver. A very common decoration on silver during the 18th century.

PEDESTAL — a trumpet- or spool-shaped stem or foot. This is a classically inspired form.

PLATE — the English word, derived from Spanish, for solid silver and bearing no relationship to the similar term "plated silver." The word "plate" was used in America during the 18th century. It fell into disuse in the 19th century, when new methods of plating and the increased availability of plated silver led to confusion.

PLATED SILVER — base metal to which a thin coating of silver has been applied, creating a less expensive substitute for solid silver.

PLINTH — a square, rectangular, oval, or octagonal base with vertical sides from which the pedestal foot of a piece rises.

PUNCH — the name of a tool, also sometimes called a die, used to impress a design into silver when struck with a hammer. Silversmiths and retailers of silver used punches with their names or initials to identify their wares. Such identifying letters are called marks or, sometimes, punches.

REEDING — molding of uniform convex shapes resembling a bundle of reeds. An especially popular form of decoration during the neoclassical period.

REPOUSSÉ — a decorative technique in which a snarling iron (an L-shaped device) is inserted into a finished piece of silver and struck, tapping out bumps on the outer surface. The bumps then may be refined into sculptural forms by chasing.

SHEFFIELD PLATING — a plating method, perfected about 1743 by Thomas Boulsover in Sheffield, England, by which a bar of copper is sandwiched between thin bars of silver and subjected to heat and pressure to create a sheet of silver-plated copper. The resulting fused sheet may be handled like a sheet of solid silver to make objects by raising or cutting, bending and soldering. Sheffield plate shows its copper core wherever it is cut. Methods to hide the inner copper have included soldering on strips of silver and pulling silver over the cut copper edge. Castings cannot be made by the Sheffield plating process. Also called fused plate.

SILVER FLATTER — a person who produces sheets of silver in a flatting mill.

STANDARD — a term referring to the adherence of a silver alloy to a specific formula, such as American coin standard, sterling standard, etc.

STERLING — the name of a specific silver alloy that is 92.5% pure silver with 7.5% copper and trace metals. The name comes from the German metallurgists of the 13th century who brought the formula to England—they were called Easterlings because Germany is east of England. In time their named was adopted for this particularly satisfactory alloy and later contracted to sterling. Although commonly used in the 20th century to mean any solid silver, the word was not usually stamped on American silver before the end of the 19th century.

TREFID SPOON — a type of spoon with a flat stem that broadens near the top and has two notches, giving the top of the stem a three-lobed shape.

TROY — a system of weight measurement traditionally used for precious metals:
  one pound troy = 12 ounces troy = 373.2 grams
  one ounce troy = 20 pennyweights (dwt.) troy = 1.097 ounce. Avoirdupois = 31.1 grams
  one pennyweight (dwt.) troy = 24 grains troy = 1.555 grams

# Select Bibliography

BANISTER, Judith. *Late Georgian and Regency Silver*. London: Country Life Books, 1971.
——. *The Country Life Collector's Pocket Book of Silver*. London: Country Life Books, 1982.

BARRETT, Geoffrey N. *Norwich Silver and Its Marks, 1565–1702*. Norwich: Wensum Press, 1981.

BENNETT, Douglas. *Irish Georgian Silver*. London: Cassell, 1972.
——. *Collecting Irish Silver, 1637–1900*. London: Souvenir Press, 1984.

BLAIR, Claude, ed. *The History of Silver*. New York: Ballantine Books, 1987.

BRETT, Vanessa. *The Sotheby's Directory of Silver, 1600–1940*. London: Sotheby's Publications, 1986.

CAMPBELL, R. *The London Tradesman*. 1747. Reprint. New York: A. M. Kelley, 1969.

CLARK, Alice. *Working Life of Women in the Seventeenth Century*. 1919. Reprint 1st ed., new impression. New York: A. M. Kelley, 1968.

CLAYTON, Michael. *The Collector's Dictionary of the Silver and Gold of Great Britain and North America*. Woodbridge, Suffolk: Antique Collectors' Club, 1973.

CULME, John. *The Directory of Gold and Silversmiths, Jewellers and Allied Traders, 1838–1914*. Woodbridge, Suffolk: Antique Collectors' Club, 1987.

DAVIS, John D. *English Silver at Williamsburg*. Williamsburg, Virginia: Colonial Williamsburg Foundation, 1976.

DEFOE, Daniel. *The Complete English Tradesman*. 2 vols., 1726. Reprint. New York: Burt Franklin, 1970.

DODD, George. *British Manufacturers: Metals*. London: Charles Knight, 1845.

EARLE, Peter. *The Making of the English Middle Class, 1660–1730*. Berkeley: University of California Press; London: Methuen, 1989.

ENSKO, Stephen G. C., and Edward WENHAM. *English Silver 1675–1825*. Rev. ed. New York: Arcadia Press, 1980.

FALLON, John P. *Marks of London Goldsmiths and Silversmiths: Georgian Period*. New York: Arco Publishing, 1972.

FLETCHER, Lucinda. *Silver*. Rev. English ed. London: Orbis Publishing, 1975.

FRASER, Antonia. *The Weaker Sex: Women's Lot in Seventeenth-Century England*. London: Methuen, 1984.

GILL, Margaret A. V. *A Directory of Newcastle Goldsmiths*. London: Worshipful Company of Goldsmiths, 1980.

GLANVILLE, Philippa. *Silver in England*. London: Unwin Hyman; Winchester, Massachusetts: Allen & Unwin, 1987.

GRIMWADE, Arthur. *Rococo Silver 1727–1765*. London: Faber, 1974.
——. *London Goldsmiths, 1697–1837: Their Marks and Lives*. 1976. Reprint. London: Faber, 1982.

GRUBER, Alain. *Silverware*. New York: Rizzoli, 1982.

HARE, Susan. *Touching Gold & Silver: 500 Years of Hallmarks*. London: Worshipful Company of Goldsmiths, 1978.

HAYWARD, John Forrest. *Huguenot Silver in England, 1688–1727*. London: Faber, 1959.
——. *The Courtauld Silver: An Introduction to the Work of the Courtauld Family of Goldsmiths*. London: Sotheby Parke Bernet Publications, 1975.

HEAL, Ambrose. *The London Goldsmiths, 1200–1800*. 1935. Reprint. Newton Abbot, Devon: David & Charles, 1972.

HELLIWELL, Stephen. *Collecting Small Silverware*. Oxford: Phaidon, 1988.

HERNMARCK, Carl. *The Art of the European Silversmith, 1430–1830*. London: Sotheby Parke Bernet Publications, 1977.

HOLLAND, Margaret. *Phaidon Guide to Silver*. Oxford: Phaidon, 1978.

HONOUR, Hugh. *Goldsmiths and Silversmiths*. New York: G. P. Putnam, 1971.

INGLIS, Brand. *The Arthur Negus Guide to British Silver*. London: Hamlyn, 1980.

JACKSON, Charles James. *An Illustrated History of English Plate, Ecclesiastical and Secular.* 1911. Reprint. New York: Dover Publications, 1969.
————. *English Goldsmiths and Their Marks.* 1905. 3rd ed., rev. and enl. *Silver & Gold Marks of England, Scotland & Ireland.* Woodbridge, Suffolk: Antique Collectors' Club, 1989.

JONES, Kenneth Crisp. *The Silversmiths of Birmingham and Their Marks, 1750–1980.* London: N. A. G. Press, 1981.

LEVER, Christopher. *Goldsmiths and Silversmiths of England.* London: Hutchinson, 1975.

LINK, Eva M. *The Book of Silver.* New York: Praeger, 1973.

LUDDINGTON, John. *Starting to Collect Silver.* Woodbridge, Suffolk: Antique Collectors' Club, 1984.

NEWMAN, Harold. *An Illustrated Dictionary of Silverware.* London: Thames and Hudson, 1987.

OMAN, Charles. *Caroline Silver, 1625–1688.* London: Faber, 1970.
————. *English Engraved Silver, 1150 to 1900.* London Faber, 1978.

PEPYS, Samuel. *The Diary of Samuel Pepys.* Edited by Robert Latham and William Matthews. 11 vols. London: Bell and Hyman, 1970–83.

PINCHBECK, Ivy. *Women Workers and the Industrial Revolution, 1750–1850.* London: G. Routledge; New York: F. S. Crofts, 1930.

PRIDEAUX, Walter Sherburne. *Memorials of The Goldsmiths' Company, Being Gleanings from Their Records between the Years 1335 and 1815.* 2 vols. London: Printed for private circulation by Eyre and Spottiswoode, 1896–97.

REDDAWAY, Thomas Fiddian, and Lorna E. M. WALKER. *The Early History of The Goldsmiths' Company, 1327–1509.* London: Arnold, 1975.

ROWE, Robert. *Adam Silver, 1765–1795.* London: Faber, 1965.

SCHRODER, Timothy B. *The Gilbert Collection of Gold and Silver.* Los Angeles: Los Angeles County Museum of Art, 1988.

SHURE, David S. *Hester Bateman, Queen of English Silversmiths.* Garden City, N. Y.: Doubleday, 1959.

SMITH, Eric J. G. "Women Silversmiths—Part I," *The Antique Dealer and Collectors' Guide,* vol. 23, no. 10 (May 1969): 67–71, 81. "Women Silversmiths—Part II: Hester Bateman," *The Antique Dealer and Collectors' Guide,* vol. 23, no. 14 (September 1969): 81–87.

VALENTINE, Nancy W. "Women Silversmiths of the 18th and 19th Centuries, Part I," *Silver,* vol. 17, no. 4 (November–December 1984): 8–15. "Women Silversmiths of the 18th and 19th Centuries, Part II," *Silver,* vol. 18, no. 1 (January–February 1985): 8–12.

WALDRON, Peter. *The Price Guide to Antique Silver.* 2nd ed. Woodbridge, Suffolk: Antique Collectors' Club, 1982.

WARK, Robert R. *British Silver in the Huntington Collection.* San Marino, California: Huntington Library, 1978.

WENHAM, Edward. "Women Recorded as Silversmiths," *The Antique Collector,* vol. 17 (March/April 1946).

WOOLLEY, Hannah. *The Gentlewoman's Companion, or a Guide to the Female Sex.* London: A. Maxwell for Edward Thomas, 1675.

WYLER, Seymour B. *The Book of Old Silver, English, American, Foreign.* New York: Crown Publishers, 1937.

YOUNG, Arthur. *A Six Months' Tour through the North of England.* 4 vols. London: W. Strahan, 1770.

# Index